SETTING UP A POTTERY WORKSHOP

Alistair Young

A & C Black · London
The American Ceramic Society

For all of my family.

First published in Great Britain 1999
A & C Black Publishers Limited
38 Soho Square
London W1D 3HB
www.acblack.com

Reprinted 2006

ISBN-10: 0-7136-7938-7
ISBN-13: 978-0-7136-7938-0

Published simultaneously in the US by
The American Ceramic Society
735 Ceramic Place
Suite 100
Westerville, Ohio 43081

ISBN: 1-57498-287-7

Copyright © 1999, 2006 Alistair Young

A CIP catalogue record for this book is available
from the British Library and from the U.S. Library
of Congress.

Illustrations
*Front cover: Firebox of a wood burning kiln, saltglaze
dishes by Alistair Young, selection of pottery tools, kiln
ready for unpacking.*
*Back cover: Walter Keeler in his workshop, photo taken
by Alistair Young.*

Frontispiece: The author's workshop,
Gloucestershire, England.

Design and typesetting by Alan Hamp

Printed and bound in China by WKT Co. Ltd

Contents

Acknowledgements

Many thanks to Linda Lambert, Jack and Joan Doherty and Simon Hulbert for their support and encouragement. Thanks also to all of the potters, from many parts of the world, who were kind enough to share information, ideas and their time to help with this book.

Introduction

Why do people become interested in the craft of pottery making today? The answers to this question are many and varied. In terms of price for everyday, utilitarian tableware the modern studio potter can no longer compete with mechanised and computerised industry, as work produced by the most skilled hand inevitably takes more time and costs more than that produced by machinery endlessly feeding production lines. Nevertheless, there is an ever-increasing number of people who rediscover the pleasures of working with clay and the satisfaction of being able to produce a unique piece of work in this age of mass production. The forms, textures and colours created in clay, whether functional, decorative or sculptural, demand a response from our senses and minds. They are made to be picked up, touched, felt and even employed in the intimacies of eating and drinking. The range of possibilities opened up by the potter's skills and processes is very wide, extending from delicate ceramic jewellery to functional domestic ware, from sculpture to architectural features, produced in workshops large and small.

This book looks at a variety of ways that these pottery workshops or studios have been set up, with examples that include details of the layout and type of work produced. The requirements of both the specialised studio and those suited for more general production are discussed. It has information for those setting up their first studio, whilst the more experienced potter will be interested in how others have developed their studios. Common processes such as the storage and preparation of materials are discussed, along with the marketing and selling of work. Also included is the production of home-made tools and equipment, which can often be made at a fraction of the cost of commercial products.

Top Outside view of Jack Troy's workshop. Photo: Jack Doherty.
Above Brook Street Pottery, Hay-on-Wye, Herefordshire, England. Photo: Simon Hulbert.

Chapter One
Workshop Planning

There will be many things to consider when deciding where to set up a pottery studio and each factor will need to be weighed against the others. The type of work which will be made will have an influence on this choice. The production thrower producing a range of large terracotta garden pots will need more space for storage of raw materials, work in progress and finished products than will someone producing small, intricately decorated porcelain pieces, resulting in a smaller volume of work. However, the latter maker will need a well-lit environment which is free from anything likely to contaminate the porcelain. Similarly, where a particular type of kiln and firing is an essential part of the making process, the choice of workshop will also be affected.

Another factor is whether the workshop will be situated in the countryside, with the possibility of a larger property, outdoor space, isolation and tranquil surroundings, or in a city location which could be compact, accessible, shared, cheap, noisy and busy.

As it is unlikely that any two potters will have the same working methods or needs, and most workshops are set up in existing buildings, some aspects of laying out a workshop are treated here

in general terms. The considerations that apply to most workshops are:
- access to the property
- access to fuel supply (this will dictate the type of firings possible)
- layout of the working area
- storage of work in progress
- the display of work for sale (only if direct selling)

In some situations choosing the ideal workshop is not possible; the workshop will need to be established in an existing or converted building, with some compromises made. There are many examples of potters successfully working from garden sheds, garages or a room within a house, but care must be taken to avoid creating any health and safety problems or breaking any town planning laws. These regulations usually classify craft pottery as a 'light industry' which is compatible with a residential area.

Jack Doherty converted a cider barn to provide a workshop where he now produces soda-glazed porcelain.

If a planning application has to be submitted for a workshop it is important that details of the proposed activity are spelt out.

- Is the equipment likely to cause more or less noise than domestic appliances?
- Will there be any industrial waste?
- Will the workshop be operating long hours each day including weekends?
- Does your raw material get delivered by large vehicles regularly?
- Local planning authorities can also be very strict about public access to retail outlets and car parking provision.

Those wanting to make most of their sales direct to the public from their workshop may need to think about how accessible the workshop is. What will attract the customer to your workshop? Selling directly to the public does have the advantage of greater profitability as the potter is not having to pay gallery or shop commissions but it will also be necessary for someone to serve the buying public. In some areas this may necessitate good parking facilities, as even the smallest business may need to accommodate more than one visitor at a time. In a central location in an established shopping area in town this may not be a problem.

If you sell all of your work at wholesale prices to galleries or shops, then the delivery of completed products must also be considered. If most sales are carried out this way and the work consists of large batches of repetition work or even smaller numbers of large individual pieces, regular collection will need to be made by a carrier.

The potters who work in suburban areas, using part of a domestic property, usually have a relatively small volume of output, focused on fewer, highly priced pieces rather than large batch production. Small amounts of materials can be brought to the workshop by car or delivered by a general carrier. Where greater production output is envisaged, reasonable access must be available for delivery. If clay is ordered by the tonne and the nearest the truck can get is 325 ft. (100 m) away, because of a narrow country lane or parked cars in a city street, an additional job of 'clay shifting' is needed. Depending on your disposition this can be looked on either as a keep-fit exercise or as an annoying interruption to the main work of making pots.

Working space

Decisions about the best layout of the workshop involve not only the overall available space but also the structural advantages and disadvantages. The space, light sources, heating and positioning of walls and doors are some of the features which can influence decisions on where to place equipment, carry out particular tasks, or store materials. Even the available space outside the workshop can affect the use of the space inside.

The amount of space needed will depend on the type of pottery made and the methods used. Throwing and hand-building both demand a different use of space. More than one type of firing may require additional space for kilns. The number of potters that will be using the workshop should be considered along with the level of production. Before taking on a workshop, work out the best use of space by planning on graph paper.

It has been estimated that one potter, working full-time in full production can operate satisfactorily in as little as 500

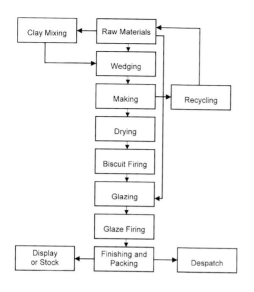

```
  Clay Mixing ────►  Raw Materials ◄─────────┐
                          │                   │
                          ▼                   │
                       Wedging                │
                          │                   │
                          ▼                   │
                        Making ──────►  Recycling
                          │                   
                          ▼                   
                        Drying                
                          │                   
                          ▼                   
                    Biscuit Firing            
                          │                   
                          ▼                   
                       Glazing ◄──────────────┘
                          │
                          ▼
                     Glaze Firing
                          │
                          ▼
  Display   ◄────  Finishing and  ──────►  Despatch
  or Stock         Packing
```

Above Ideal Workshop – Flow Diagram. Materials and products should move through the workshop with minimum difficulty.

Below Clay preparation area at Brook Street Pottery.

sq. ft. (46m²) of floor space. However this would not include any allowance for the display of finished work which may account for an additional 250–300 sq. ft. (23–28m²). In a shared workshop some saving of space will result from the sharing of equipment such as kilns, which may be used more regularly or even continuously at times. Additional storage space as well as room for wheels etc. would mean that four people would need at least 1000 sq. ft. (93m²). If a display and sales area is to be considered as well, then this would need to be considerably larger than that needed for a workshop for one person.

Distinct advantages are gained from sharing a workshop, particularly for those just starting out. Capital expenses and overheads can be shared along with ideas and varied expertise. The group can also share the cost of promotional material and hold joint exhibitions. The organisation of a shared workshop

needs to be very thorough to ensure that everyone knows exactly what their responsibilities are. Rules should be set up by the group, or the owner of the property, which state clearly how the workshop will run, including the financial liabilities of each member.

An ideal plan for the layout of a workshop would provide for the easy flow of materials from storage, through production, firing, packing and despatch or display of the finished products. This flow of materials should avoid the lifting and moving of the same items back and forth. It should also prevent the accumulation of materials in such a way that they have to be moved in order to gain access to other items. Objects can also become a hazard in the workshop if stored in areas, which are used as pathways. These should be kept free to allow the easy movement of people and often fragile work.

Clay mixing

If clay mixing is to be carried out in the workshop then it is best situated in an area which is separate from the main production space, to avoid the spread of dust. Most clay mixing equipment produces a considerable amount of noise, which can be a nuisance if there is more than one person using the workshop. Clay mixing should also be carried out as near as possible to where the clay materials are stored to avoid unnecessary movement of heavy weights. The equipment used in this process, and the clay itself, is heavy and needs a substantial floor to bear their combined weight. Dust extraction is necessary to remove dust-laden air from the work area.

Where the technique of clay mixing results in a semi-liquid or slip that needs to be dried out, space must be allowed for this. Some method of warming the room will be helpful in colder climates although good ventilation is a very important part of the process, allowing the hot, damp air to be removed.

If a dough mixer is used, the resulting clay body is often too soft to use without some drying. This is normally done by forming thick clay arches that are stood in a row so that the air can circulate around them. The space needed for these processes will depend on the volume to be dried.

Wedging

If possible the clay should be stored near the wedging bench which should be positioned on a floor which is strong enough to bear the constant pounding of clay. The bench itself should be sturdily built from heavy timber with an absorbent surface of marine plywood, or constructed from brick with a concrete top which has been finished to a smooth surface by repeated polishing with a plasterer's float. The height is a very important factor and should be calculated so that the back can be kept as straight as possible when picking the clay up or kneading, whilst allowing sufficient room to drop and slam the clay together, if using the slicing method. Wedging benches are often too high off the ground.

Production

The main production area should be situated close to the clay store and drying area. Good lighting is very important for overall illumination, with additional lighting over workbenches or wheels. Shelving should be arranged close to the wheel or hand-building

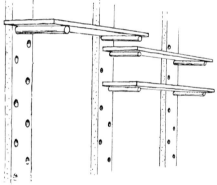

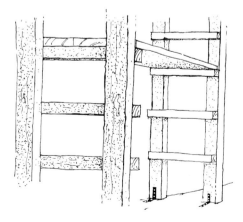

Above Shelving System. Whichford Pottery, Warwickshire, England.

Left Shelving Systems. A good shelving system will accommodate pots of different heights. Second-hand timber can be used, but make sure that it is strong. Remember that these shelves can hold a lot of work when full.

bench so that finished work can be placed there without the need to move from the work area. A flexible shelving system should be used which will hold removable boards so that when the boards are filled they can be moved to a drying area or onto the next stage in the process. The system should also allow for work of varying heights to be stored easily. Mobile shelf units can be very useful as they allow the work to be moved between specialist work areas.

A water supply is an essential part of all clay forming techniques, ideally a sink with both hot and cold water. Care must be taken to prevent blocking the drainage system with clay slurry and also to prevent potentially hazardous glaze materials contaminating the water supply. Several methods are available to control these problems. A clay trap could be installed under the sink. This comprises of a tank which permits water to flow through, whilst allowing the solid particles to settle out of the water and sink to the bottom of the tank. Alternatively, a settling tank or pit can be constructed outside the workshop, using porous materials which will allow the water to seep through, leaving a residue which can be cleaned out at regular intervals. Another simple way of dealing with the problem is to pour any water which has clay or glaze in it into a large bucket in the sink. The heavy materials will settle and the clean water can be poured off the top. The residue can then be taken out and disposed of in a safe manner.

Weekly washing of workshop floors is

Walter Keeler uses a wood stove to speed up the drying of some pots. Photo: Jack Doherty

Clay Trap. A 15 gal. (68 l.) water tank is used for this settling tank. The type which includes a reinforcing ridge down the side are the easiest to use. A rigid plastic or aluminium sheet should be fixed to the side nearest the incoming water. Another sheet of similar material can be suspended on the other side of the ridge. When water travels from the first chamber into the second, it will be first deflected downwards, before pushing clean water through the outlet.

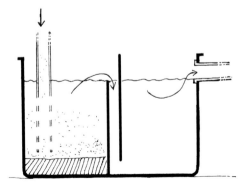

good practice and will minimise dust; floor drains will facilitate this. However, the clay/water mix should go into a clay trap before entering any main drainage system.

Heating will be required in most climates. It is important to maintain a comfortable room heat to enable efficient production, as the effect of cold on the hands when working with water and wet clay can be most painful. It is also essential to prevent the temperature dropping below freezing during the night or when the workshop is not being used. Frost will ruin any damp work and spoil unused clay and must be avoided if possible. Completed work will need to dry at a steady rate in order to keep the production flowing. This will be more of

14

At Whichford Pottery completed pots are stacked on the slatted floor over the kiln room to dry. Warm air is also carried by metal ducting to other parts of the workshop.

a problem in some climates or at certain times of the year, but drying pots will benefit from a well-heated workshop. Beware of heat sources such as portable butane or oil heaters which produce a considerable quantity of moisture as well as heat.

It is possible to utilise heat produced by kilns to dry pots. If the main production area is on the first floor, the area above the kilns can be fitted with a slatted floor which allows warm air to rise through the pots. Obviously this is most effective if the firings are carried out on a regular basis. Ducting can also be installed to carry warm air to other parts of the workshop, but the main problem with this system is that the heat may also carry airborne dust with it, increasing the health and safety risk.

Firing

The safe siting and operation of kilns is discussed at the end of Chapter 4. It is preferable that kilns are not sited in the general production area without good ventilation, as they often emit fumes during the firing. Kilns are sometimes located in outbuildings or even domestic garages and this can be a good solution provided that there is no petrol present, either stored or in cars, because of the danger from the flammable vapour it gives off. All other combustible materials should also be kept well away. If the kiln is situated in the workshop ensure that there is adequate ventilation as described in the section on kilns.

A position near the drying shelves will assist the drying of pots and facilitate the flow of work. Space should be allowed for the storage of kiln furniture. Shelves and props can easily be broken if knocked over or dropped and are expensive to replace. The safest way to store kiln shelves is by standing

Glaze-mixing and decorating area in Richard Godfrey's workshop. Glaze materials are stored in large plastic boxes with lids, previously used for catering packs of ice cream.

them on edge in a rack. If they are laid flat, one on another, the combined weight is likely to break the bottom shelf.

Glazing

The amount of space allocated specifically for glazing may depend on the emphasis placed on this process by the potter. Glazing can be carried out on a general purpose workbench and if a single glaze is kept for all work, then very little dedicated space may be necessary. If pots are to be decorated with detailed brushwork, a dedicated decorating area would be important, with access to natural light if possible, and areas where brushes and colours can be stored.

A mobile shelving system can be very

useful to move biscuited work near to the glazing area. Alternatively, an area used specifically for glazing could include shelving and work surfaces. These should be made of non-porous materials which are easy to wipe clean, and low enough to hold glaze bins at a convenient working height. Glaze materials can also be stored nearby, within easy reach for glaze mixing and the preparation of glaze tests. Each material should be labelled clearly with its name, whether it is toxic or hazardous, and whether particular precautions need to be taken when used.

Packing finished work

When glaze kilns are unpacked, a clean space is needed to lay out the work for inspection. Pots are examined for quality, and stoneware pieces may need to be ground to smooth off roughness on bases. Earthenware pieces which have been fired with the use of stilts need to be handled with the utmost care

in case the stilts have left behind razor sharp pieces of glass. If a power grinder is used, then eye protection must be worn by everyone in the vicinity because of the danger of flying chips of glaze or pottery.

Work which has been made to order should be wrapped and packed for dispatch. The amount of packaging depends on the method of transport but it is better to be on the safe side when sending work by carrier. Wrapping materials should be light but strong, giving support to the work throughout its journey. Bubble wrap is good when used in several layers, although care must be taken when wrapping large pieces or packing work at the bottom of large crates, as the bubbles do burst, leaving two sheets of polythene which give little protection. Foam paper is probably one of the best materials available although it is expensive. Polystyrene chips are good as a back-up packing to pots which have some wrapping already, but they do have to be

Mobile shelves save time when moving pots and equipment around the workshop. This unit, made by Richard Godfrey, is based on a trolley used by bakers to move trays of bread.

placed carefully so that there is a good layer of chips between the pieces of work. They tend to take up more room than wrapping materials alone. If weight is not a consideration, then corrugated card is an excellent packing material as it is strong and does not crush very easily. It is worth looking out for a supply of second-hand packing materials from industry or business, as it is often treated as a waste product by companies who regularly receive carefully wrapped components. A cheap and effective home-made packaging can be made from supermarket carrier bags filled with crumpled paper, cloth or other available material. These bags are sealed with tape and positioned to separate the pots inside the box. Good packing material is essential for the safe transportation of work but it is very bulky and takes up an extraordinary amount of storage space.

Strong cardboard boxes, such as those used to carry computers and televisions, are suitable for small- to medium-sized work, but wooden cases must be considered for larger sculptural work. When the box has been packed full, allowing additional material around the side, top and bottom, the top should be secured with strong packing tape. Make sure that the box cannot distort so that the packing material will settle and allow the pots to touch. Mark the boxes as 'fragile'.

It is worth asking other potters to recommend a good carrying company. There are some who specialise in moving artwork and sculpture. Delivering work yourself is a good way to meet buyers and galleries, as well as having a day out of the workshop.

Display

If the finished pots are to be displayed for sale from the workshop, they will need to be checked and finished in the same way. How they are to be displayed will depend very much on the type of work and the preferences and tastes of the potter. Work which is closely related in form and surface, such as repetition domestic ware, may be best seen in multiples, or as groups of objects, so as to stress the themes running throughout the work. Each piece is then seen as part of a series, or of the range of work as a whole. Pots which have a more individual nature, such as sculptural forms or individual pots, will need more

Left Display of ceramics by Jane Hamlyn at the Collection gallery, Ledbury, England.

Below Richard Godfrey's showroom.

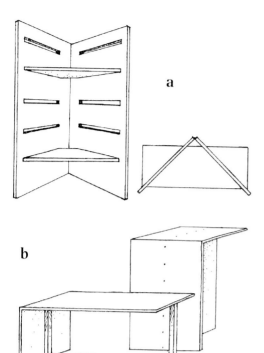

a

b

Display Stands

(a) For situations where temporary displays have to be set up quickly, such as at potters' markets, this type of design is easy to operate. The vertical boards are hinged at the back and can also be made with three panels, in a 'U' shape with slots cut in both side panels. Boards can be of MDF, blockboard or plywood. Shelves can be of the same or of solid timber or glass.

(b) These stands can be used in many different configurations. Made from almost any sheet board, they can include a wooden frame support or another sheet of board. If they need to be dismantled regularly, special screw fittings are available which do not wear with use. Display stands should be designed to enhance the qualities of the work on display.

Jack Doherty's display area for porcelain.

space in which to establish their identity. The form will be most clearly seen against a plain background and there should be room for the spectator to move around the piece to view it from each side.

As pottery is usually on quite a small scale, the height of display surfaces is an important consideration. If the side profile is an important feature of a piece then it should be positioned so that the spectator can view it without getting down on the floor. It is much easier to view individual small pots at 3-4 ft. (0.9-1.2 m) above the ground, on raised plinths or showcases. Even with the work raised to a viewing point which suits its scale, it may be necessary to vary the height of each piece, particularly if they are all of a similar size, by using simple blocks or display stands. The careful arrangement of groups of pieces can help demonstrate particular features of the work.

Lighting is always a very important feature in the display of pottery. Good lighting will enhance the form, surface texture and colour of the work. A focused beam from a spotlight will give the variation in surface light and shade which emphasises the form more than diffused fluorescent lighting. The display area should have plenty of adjustable spotlights so that they can be altered to suit different displays.

Safe workshop practice – general

- There are always potential dangers in any workplace where equipment and tools are used and the potter must be aware of those lurking in their own workshop. When planning your workshop try to design for safety, and anticipate possible difficult areas.
- Will you be able to move freely about the work area without walking into equipment or furniture?
- Will you have to carry heavy materials up and down stairs? Can they be stored at waist height to avoid bending? Can wheels or castors be employed to reduce the risk of muscle injury?
- Is there a potential fire hazard from heat from the kiln?
- How will you protect the public from potential dangers?
- When the workshop is running, a regular assessment of all aspects of health and safety should be planned and undertaken. A Health and Safety officer could visit at any time.
- What precautions will be taken to reduce dust? Specialist vacuum cleaner with specified dust filters may be used or floors washed with a down hose.

Chapter Two
Materials

Clay mixing and recycling

An extensive range of prepared clay bodies is available from pottery material suppliers; these clays are successfully used by a great many potters, and may be blended together to alter their handling and firing characteristics. Other potters prefer to have complete control of these properties by preparing their own clay bodies from a blend of powdered raw materials, or from a naturally occurring source. This enables the body to be adjusted to suit the requirements for both making and firing. Recipes can be developed to produce clay of a particular colour, firing temperature, strength, texture, shrinkage etc.

The economics of preparing your own clay can be argued either way. The cost of clay bodies produced this way is often from one third to one half that of comparable commercial bodies. A saving is also made in delivery costs, as prepared bodies contain a considerable weight of water. On the other hand the actual weighing and mixing of the clay body can be very time consuming, and the raw materials are also bulky and need to be stored in a dry place. Thought should be given to the relative advantages and disadvantages before embarking on this route.

Preparing clay bodies from raw materials

Small quantities of clay body can be prepared without the use of complicated equipment. Amounts up to 55 lb. (25 kg.) can be reasonably handled at one time but there are two considerations to be taken into account. Dry clay materials need extra large weighing scales to cope with the volume of material and care must be taken not to create airborne dust which can be a health hazard.

Powdered ingredients should be added to water in a suitable container and stirred by hand or with an electric mixer. When mixed to an even consistency, the clay slurry is poured first through a 20s mesh, then a 60s mesh sieve. Finely ground clays from a commercial supplier can be put through a 100s mesh sieve. Drying can be carried out on plaster or other porous board. Alternatively, the clay slurry can be poured into cloth bags which allow the water to seep through the fabric fibres, retaining the clay. The bags should be supported in weld-mesh boxes or wooden trays with expanded metal or weld-mesh bases, and allowed to drip. Soft clay can be dried further by fashioning it into thick rolls which will stand up when bent into arches. This allows air to flow around the damp clay, thus speeding up the drying process.

Commercial clay mixers

In the USA, commercially produced mixers are available, such as the Soldner Clay Mixer which consists of a round concrete bowl revolving around fixed blades which do the mixing. The concrete bowl prevents the clay sticking and can be used to store plastic clay after mixing. Another type, produced by Bluebird Engineering, uses a horizontal-rotating shaft with blades at the bottom of a container. This mixer allows the operator to tip out the contents when the process is complete.

Dough mixers

Bakers' dough mixers make excellent clay mixers and may sometimes be purchased secondhand when no longer suitable for dough making. They are usually of strong construction with a powerful electric motor, which drives the mixing arm and revolves the mixing bowl. Although the original purpose

Above Dough mixers can be very efficient clay mixers. This one will mix 330 lb. (150 kg.) in about 30 minutes. The lid has been fitted with a strip of polythene to reduce the amount of dust produced.

Below Bluebird Engineering's clay mixer. Photo: Bluebird Engineering.

Filter press at the Whichford Pottery.

Filter presses and pan mills

was to add air to the dough mix, most designs actually cut and compress the clay so that the ingredients are blended together efficiently. A measured amount of water is poured into the mixer first, to reduce the amount of dust produced when the powdered ingredients are added. The less plastic materials like china clay can be improved by adding them first and allowing them to form a slip. Sizes vary from those that can take about 55 lb. (25 kg.) up to 275 lb.(125 kg.) of materials and water per operation. Clay bodies produced by this method benefit from being kept for some time before being used. Two things occur during this time which improves the plasticity. The fine particles used in the mix become thoroughly wetted and the clay becomes slightly more acidic. Adding vinegar or even stale wine to the mix can help speed up this action.

In the ceramics industry, clay bodies are produced by two main methods. The first entails blending powdered clays in slip form in a blunger, which stirs the measured ingredients together. The slip is then pumped under pressure into a filter press, which consists of a series of hollow metal plates lined with cloth. The cloth is tightly clamped between the plates so that water can be forced out whilst the clay is retained inside. When the plates are unclamped, the plastic body can be peeled from the filter cloths. The second process involves crushing lump clay by passing it through a pan mill. Both of these processes require heavy equipment which is usually too large and expensive for one person working alone, but small versions are made for laboratory use and these are of use to those potters who require greater control over their clay body production.

Pugmills

A pugmill is used to reconstitute clay. It consists of a series of blades arranged in a spiral along a shaft, which revolves within a cylinder. When clay is put into the pugmill it is chopped and compressed as it passes through, until it emerges as a sausage. Clay bodies produced in a dough mixer are often of an open texture and can be improved by being passed through a pugmill. When clay has been recycled it can be processed by a pugmill to bring it back to an even consistency. Sand and grog may be added to a clay body or two different clay bodies may be blended. Soft and firm clay can be blended together to produce the required consistency.

The standard device does not perform all of the functions of hand wedging and pockets of air are often trapped in the clay. To remove this, the de-airing pugmill has a vacuum pump attached which sucks the air out as it travels through. This is a very useful item of equipment, both for getting new clay into condition and for reconditioning old clay. Clay, which has been mechanically mixed temporarily loses some of its plasticity, and may need to be stored for several weeks before it returns to its optimum condition.

Some potters increase the versatility of the pugmill as a production tool by adding die plates on to the outlet to produce extruded forms such as coils for hand building and flat tiles or sheets of clay. Repetition throwers can cut measured pieces of clay as it appears from the machine, using a tool to measure sections of extruded clay. This method can quickly produce pieces of clay of the same weight ready for throwing.

The rate of output from a pugmill can be an important factor for a production potter and should be considered before a purchase is made. Manufacturers often specify an amount of clay that can be processed per hour but it is advisable to check this information with someone using the same model in a workshop situation, as the output may be different in practice from laboratory tests.

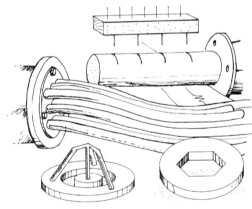

Above Pugmill Attachments. A pugmill can be a versatile tool in the workshop. Measured sections of clay can be a quick way of producing particular weights of clay for batch production. Dies can be fitted for extruding coils and other pre-formed clay shapes.

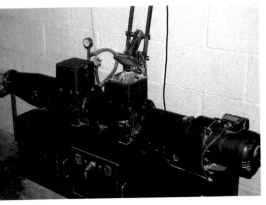

Left A de-airing pugmill used for porcelain clay by Jack Doherty.

Clay storage

Make sure that the floor that you intend to store the clay on is strong enough to take the weight of the clay. A tonne of clay may be too much for a wooden floor designed to take the weight of humans and not much more. Access is also important, as valuable time can be wasted carrying bags of clay up stairs or along corridors, as well as putting the person carrying the heavy weight at risk of injury. A trolley or sack truck is essential to move heavy loads wherever possible.

Plastic sheeting is the ideal material in which to store prepared clay, which if wrapped carefully, will stay damp almost indefinitely provided it is kept out of direct sunlight and frost. The sunlight has the effect of breaking down the plastic which quickly becomes fragile and frost causes the moisture in the clay to freeze into pieces of ice, breaking down the structure of the clay and drying out some areas whilst softening others. Clay that has been frosted must be re-mixed and wedged to an even consistency or it will cause many problems throughout the making process.

Clay bodies improve with age and become more pliable and plastic in use. A freshly mixed batch of clay is always less plastic than the same body which has been stored for at least three months or even a year. This process is called souring or ageing and it happens for two reasons. In a clay body which has been prepared from powdered clay, it takes time for the added water to penetrate the finest particles and wet them thoroughly. The other factor is the gradual change from slight alkalinity to a more acidic state, caused by the growth of minute organisms in the clay.

These changes will bring the clay body to its optimum state but will not convert a poor body into a good one.

A cool, dark, damp room with little airflow through it would be the ideal place to store and age clay. In Fiji they wrap clay in banana leaves, dig a hole in the ground and store it for up to three months.

Clay recycling

Although some potters find that it is more economical to throw away their scrap clay the recycling of clay has always been part of the potter's craft and most workshops have some facility for this activity.

Systems for recycling clay can be simple and inexpensive. An old bath or plastic dustbin can be used for soaking down the ingredients which are then dried either in the sun, on blocks of porous plaster, or in biscuit-fired bowls. More sophisticated equipment may be needed to process larger amounts. Drying trays can be made from firebricks or kiln shelves and heated by gas burners. If cloth is used to line a drying trough, the fibres in the fabric can assist the drying through capillary action and without the use of heat. If the cloth is allowed to hang down below the level of the clay then the water can siphon away and drip on to the floor. Plaster-topped tables can be inlaid with the type of electric heating elements normally used in greenhouses to warm the soil. This not only speeds up the drying by heating the clay, but will also continue to dry out the plaster after use, preparing it for the next batch of wet clay.

These practices reflect the view that materials should be conserved and treated with respect. However, if the time taken to recycle materials is costed it can work out to be an expensive undertaking, particularly with the less expensive commercial bodies. For those who prepare their own clay body from raw ingredients, it is of course less of a problem, as the wetted scraps can be added to the next mix. In fact the addition of wet throwing scraps from the wheel will often improve the plasticity of a freshly mixed body.

Glaze materials

Most potters today have access to a wide range of prepared raw materials and even prepared glazes. The scope of these prepared glazes is, however, limited when compared with the amazing variety of effects which can be achieved by experimenting with materials to develop new and individual glazes. The range can be further extended in some cases by the use of naturally occurring materials which have not been processed and purified to industrial standards.

Many key materials can be obtained from local sources, often at a fraction of the cost of commercial suppliers. An understanding of basic glaze chemistry and the geology of your local area will tell you what to look for and where. Investigate any businesses which use earth materials. Clay pits or brick works may provide a variety of clays suitable for glaze recipes, or decorating slips, even if they are not suitable for making pots. Granite, marble, limestone and sandstone quarries each provide waste material which is worth testing, especially those with stone crushing plants producing quantities of stone dust. These may make an unusual contribution to your glazes. The fine dust may be collected in dust extraction units or found settled on ledges in the crushing plant. Check with the company first, who may be willing to help with this unusual request for their waste product. Alternatively it may be worth calcining rocks such as granite by heating slowly to a red heat in a kiln. On cooling, the pieces are soft enough to be crumbled by hand.

Wood ash is an example of a glaze material which is readily available and, when prepared in small quantities, often contains traces of impurities which enhance the fired glaze. Rivers often expose underlying materials through erosion, so take samples from river banks or river mud and carry out tests.

Sources of useful materials are not limited to rural areas however and many interesting ingredients can be found in the city. Look for manufacturing processes with waste products such as metal grinding, which may produce iron filings or brass filings, from a factory or even a key cutting machine in a high street store. These samples may also include traces of silicon carbide from the grinding wheel; this will also affect the glaze. Rusting steel can give a coarse iron oxide with different decorative properties from the finer industrial grades.

The main limitation on the use of 'found' materials is the need to reduce them to a fine powder if they are to be mixed into a glaze suspension. This is very labour intensive and, when added to the time taken to find and collect the material and carry out tests, it can become uneconomical. Some materials will be too hard to break down without the use of expensive equipment, but it may be possible to find a source of fine powder which is the result of another industrial process.

Storing glaze materials

Powdered glaze materials, whether purchased from a pottery supplies company or processed by the potter, need to be kept in clearly labelled, air-tight containers. This will allow easy access whilst creating the minimum amount of dust. The paper and plastic sacks which are used by the suppliers should only be considered as temporary storage. Plastic containers are often available from businesses and factories which would normally throw them away. Caterers use giant ice cream containers with snap-on lids, chemists throw away screw-top plastic containers, builders use and discard plastic buckets of paint and other materials. Provided they can be easily cleaned, these will make excellent storage for glaze materials, mixed glazes, ceramic colours and slips. Steel drums are prone to rusting and can spoil glaze ingredients by contamination with iron unless thick plastic sacks are used to line them first. If the storage containers are placed on staging or racking above floor level, any spillage can be cleaned away easily.

Where space is limited, bulky materials can be stored under work surfaces in purpose-built containers

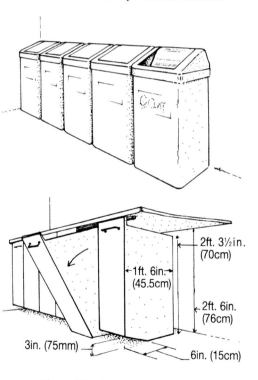

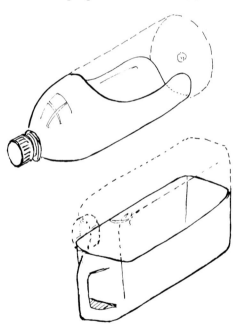

Top Plastic litter bins with swing tops.
Above Glaze material storage. This system can be adjusted to fit existing work benches. The boxes should be big enough to hold a full sack of material and the sides and back of the bench need to be covered to prevent dust escaping into the room.

Scoops for powdered glaze materials are easily cut from strong plastic containers with stout scissors or knife. It is a good idea to make one for each container of glaze material. This prevents cross-contamination from dirty scoops. An effective funnel for pouring liquids can be made by cutting the top ⅓ off with a straight cut.

designed to take a sack of powder. These boxes are made from plywood and have a cut away base which allows them to be tipped forward in use. Some materials of similar weight take up more space than others, and containers can be built to different dimensions to accommodate this. A good seal can be made by extending the front of the container up to the edge of the work surface.

To avoid cross-contamination of materials it is useful to have a scoop for each of the materials used, kept in each storage container. These can be made from empty plastic, beer or lemonade bottles, cut so that the necks form handles.

Safe workshop practice – materials

Clay

- This is a combination of alumina and silica and along with other materials containing silica, can cause silicosis, a respiratory disease caused by the inhalation of silica dust. This is often of a very fine particle size, which can be suspended in the air for many hours and has an accumulative effect on the lungs over a period of time. Dust is created wherever clay is allowed to dry and is subject to abrasion.
- Work surfaces should be sponged regularly to prevent a build-up of dust. Floors should be sealed and level and may be cleaned with a vacuum cleaner with a suitable high efficiency three-stage filter, or mopped. Mopping must be thorough and include repeated rinses to avoid spreading a thin layer of clay over the entire floor. Avoid sweeping as it only stirs up the dust.
- Work clothes or overalls should be made of synthetic fibres that do not hold clay dust so readily as natural fibres. They should be washed regularly and not worn in living areas.
- Clay should be stored and mixed in a separate room. Bags of dry clay and other ceramic materials should be stacked on pallets or some other heavy shelving off the floor to aid cleaning. Clay mixers should be fitted both with a cover to reduce the amount of dust escaping, and a dust extraction system. A suitable dust mask should be worn if these precautions are not fully effective.
- Take care when lifting bags of clay and other materials, and always lift with knees bent. Back problems can often be traced to poor lifting or posture at work. Standing rather than sitting at the wheel can be a help. Repetitive work can cause carpal tunnel syndrome in wrists so aim to vary your working position and take breaks regularly.
- It is good practice to wear an appropriate dust mask when handling any powders. Materials containing silica include: clay bodies, china clay, ball clay, bentonite, Cornish stone, feldspars, flint, frits, quartz, talc and woolastonite.
- Extraction fans should be used near any dry fettling processes.

Glaze and colouring materials

- These materials are classed as toxic because of their effect on the human system. The poisonous nature of these materials varies greatly but most of them can be harmful whether they have been inhaled as dust, ingested through the digestive system, or through cuts or abrasions in the skin.

- Lead compounds in most countries are regulated through legislation, due to the hazard of lead poisoning which has an accumulative effect on the body, particularly the nervous system. Lead in all forms, fritted as well as raw, is a harmful material and potters must take great care when handling it in the workshop.
- Lead frits are dangerous if inhaled or ingested but lead and other metals can also be leached from fired ware (particularly low-fired or under-fired) that comes into contact with an acid such as fruit juice, coffee or tomato juice. Continual use in a microwave is also thought to increase the amount of metal released. The metals in question are derived from lead compounds, cadmium and selenium compounds, antimony oxide, arsenic oxide, barium carbonate, copper oxide and carbonate, chromium oxide, potassium dichromate and zinc oxide.
- Fired glazes can be tested in the laboratory for solubility which must be below a maximum statutory level, measured in parts per million, which varies in different countries. Be aware of local regulations when using these materials on functional pottery and have the finished work tested by a recognised testing laboratory. Glazes which contain materials that may be hazardous should only be used on clearly non-functional work and should be handled and stored with great care. There are other risks attached to the use of fired, lead-glazed objects: these are discussed in the section on leaching from fired glazes.
- When mixing glazes, reduce dust as much as possible by adding materials to water – wet glazes are not a dust hazard. Other fluxes such as barium and lithium are highly toxic when inhaled, so use an extraction system and wear an approved toxic dust mask. Spillages should be mopped up as soon as possible and gloves should be worn when handling wet or dry glazes.
- Glazes and colouring materials should never be sprayed without the use of an efficient extractor fan that collects the over-sprayed glaze in either a filter or a water curtain. These are expensive items to buy, but you can make efficient alternatives for your workshop (see the diagrams on page 35).

Chapter Three
Workshop Equipment

The choice of equipment will depend on both the type of work that the potter will be making and the funds available. Some potters choose to keep the amount of mechanical equipment in their workshop to a minimum, preferring to work the clay by hand through each stage of the process. For example, one person may prepare the clay by wedging, use a kick wheel, simple hand tools and complete the work in a wood-fired kiln. It is possible to work successfully without depending on expensive equipment which can bring accompanying problems of noise, maintenance and, often, the need for professional repair. Simple but effective hand tools can also be made quite easily from cheap or recycled materials.

Other potters may take the view that some equipment can speed up the making process and reduce the more mundane or physical work. This saving of time may enable them to produce work which is more competitively priced and profitable.

Workbenches

A basic item for all workshops must be a sturdy workbench. If the work is hand-built it may be necessary to stand or sit at the bench for long periods of time and the correct height is very important for comfortable working conditions. Strong benches are not usually adjustable so try working at different levels before settling on one, and if the height needed to stand and work is then too high to sit at, use an adjustable draughtsman's or high typist's chair. These give additional support to the back.

Turntables and whirlers

Each time a clay object is picked up and turned around joins can be stressed, forms distorted and surfaces disrupted by often unwanted fingermarks. A turntable will allow work to be carried out freely on even the largest or most fragile of pieces and allow the piece to be easily viewed from all sides.

The turntables available from craft pottery suppliers usually have a top and base of about 9 in. (23 cm) diameter. The circular base is fitted with a simple 'bush' bearing and the flat top has a shaft which fits into it. These are suitable for most uses but are probably too small for wide, asymmetrical pieces of work which can tip over. If wider turntables are unavailable the standard model can be adapted by fixing a larger wooden or metal disc to the top and base to give added stability. Very large sculptural or architectural works may need a turntable consisting of a square or round board fitted with a number of castors around the edge.

Whirlers are similar to turntables except that they have heavier tops, usually plaster of Paris cast on to the central spindle. They were originally used for press-moulding, as momentum will keep them turning slowly and steadily, freeing both hands to work on the mould.

Turntables and whirlers can easily be made from steel or wood and simple bearings to suit individual requirements.

Potters' wheels

The potter's wheel has taken a variety of forms through history, from the Japanese hand momentum wheel to the continental momentum and geared kick wheels developed in Europe. The electric power wheel is a development of these principles, but the basic requirements of any wheel are that the wheelhead must run true, without wobble or vibration. It must withstand heavy pressure downwards and at an angle, and the operator must have control over the speed.

Momentum wheels

The simplest kind of wheel is the momentum wheel which consists of a heavy flywheel mounted on a shaft supported by a bearing. These wheels are silent in operation and require the thrower to have an economy of action as a response to the falling momentum of the flywheel. The clay needs to be coaxed with this type of wheel rather than forced or driven as with a power wheel. Exponents of momentum wheels claim that they add subtle qualities to the pots.

Oriental-style momentum wheels have a heavy flywheel, which also forms the wheelhead. A stick is inserted into a deep hole drilled into the outer edge of the wheel in order to rotate it, and a rhythm develops as the potter alternates between spinning the wheel and

throwing. The potter may sit cross-legged in front of the wheel.

With the continental momentum wheel a large flywheel is set at the bottom of a shaft and a light wheelhead is fixed to the top. This arrangement is usually mounted in a wooden frame which includes a bench seat, thereby allowing the operator's legs to swing from the knee in order to kick the wheel round, leaving both hands free to work the clay. The frame can also provide a good surface for placing tools and thrown pots.

Concrete is frequently used to provide weight for the flywheel and, if this is distributed around the outer edge, makes starting the wheel easier than one which is completely solid, without reducing the momentum.

Kick wheels

Kick wheels have a geared crank which allows the potter to drive the flywheel by pushing a horizontal bar backwards and forwards by foot. The operation is very similar to the continental momentum wheel, with the advantage that the

Soldner wheel, Bluebird (USA). This type of wheel enables the potter to stand and apply weight when centering large weights of clay.

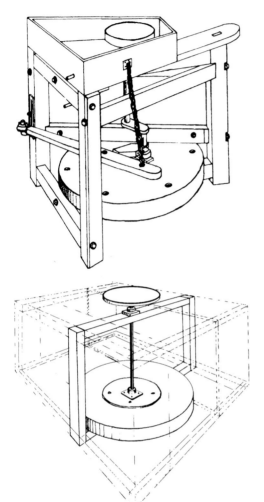

'Leach-type' kick wheel and momentum wheel.

geared kick bar can allow constant and higher speeds. With practice it is possible to throw large and small pieces with this type of wheel, it is virtually silent and has many of the advantages of the momentum wheel. It is important that a seat is provided, and that the kick bar is adjustable to suit the operator, in order to maintain a constant speed. Kick wheels without seats are not easy to use and are not recommended.

Momentum and kick wheels are available from potters' equipment manufacturers but can also be made from scratch without extensive skills, using simple tools. The shaft may need to be welded at one end to accommodate the crank, and machined at the other to take the wheelhead.

Electric wheels

There are many different types of electrically-powered wheels on the market, but they fall into two main categories based on the arrangement for controlling the speed. Those in the first category have a d.c. (direct current) motor with an electronic control for adjusting the speed, and the motor is usually connected to the main shaft with a drive belt. This method gives a smooth increase and decrease in speed, relatively quiet operation and good control particularly at low speeds. Some potters have built their own electric wheel using this principle because it requires few components although d.c. motors can be an expensive item.

The second category contains wheels with mechanical methods of controlling the speed. This category tends to be noisier and less controllable at low speeds but possibly easier to repair as the mechanics are fairly simple and any faults are usually clear to see.

Electric wheels also vary in power and this will affect the amount of clay that can be thrown on them. For regular, general uses an electric motor of at least $1/3$ hp would be a minimum with $1/2$ hp or above, preferable for constant use and large pieces. Large quantities of clay thrown on a wheel that is under-powered will slow down the motor, which may then be damaged by overloading.

The late Mick Casson throwing on a Raefco wheel with a d.c. drive.

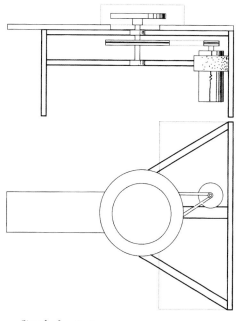

Simple d.c. System.

Ergonomics

Potters who spend a long time throwing may find that they develop aches and pains because of the way that they have to adapt to the shape of the wheel. Backache is very common and may be caused by working in the sitting position, which forces the thrower to use the back muscles when applying pressure to the clay. A wheel with an adjustable or separate seat is an advantage. Those which allow the potter to stand and work, permit him to use his body weight to lean down on the clay, particularly when centering.

Similarly care must be taken with any process which requires working in one position for a long time. Make sure that the work is at the best height and supported on a turntable or whirler if possible. Take regular breaks away from the work and vary your work.

Extruders

Very useful tools for producing a variety of forms such as handles, hollow shapes and profiles. Simple to make from scrap metal cylinders or tubes, they can greatly assist production and are used extensively by potters such as John Glick (USA) and John Alliston and David Frith (UK).

Spray guns

Richard Godfrey has made an effective but inexpensive spray gun. Based on an air 'gun' supplied by motor factors for use in the motor repair trade, it operates on the principle of an artist's diffuser, used to spray fixative onto drawings. It is adjustable, easily cleaned, and uses throwaway plastic containers as reservoirs. As there are no moving parts

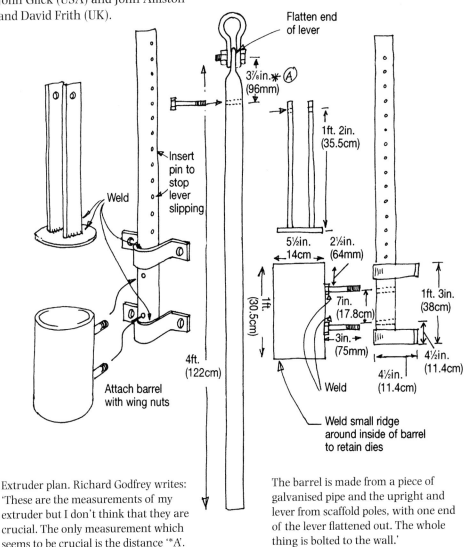

Extruder plan. Richard Godfrey writes: 'These are the measurements of my extruder but I don't think that they are crucial. The only measurement which seems to be crucial is the distance '*A'.

The barrel is made from a piece of galvanised pipe and the upright and lever from scaffold poles, with one end of the lever flattened out. The whole thing is bolted to the wall.'

in contact with abrasive glaze or slip particles it does not wear out in the same way as the commercial brands. When spraying several different glazes or pigments it is easy to switch from one to another by changing containers and it can be cleaned by simply blowing

water through the spray.

When spraying, a suitable dust mask must be worn at all times and care should be taken to contain the overspray which could present a health hazard. Spraying is usually carried out in a

Left Spray gun design by Richard Godfrey. The spray is produced by a diffuser, of the type used to fix charcoal drawings, or made from copper tubing fixed into a wooden block. With no other moving parts there is little chance of blockage. The gun part of this spray allows the air to be turned on and off and can be bought very cheaply from garage equipment stockists or air-powered tool manufacturers. The diameter of the spray jet can be adjusted by experimenting with the relative position of the tubes. Photo: Richard Godfrey

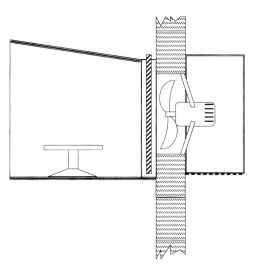

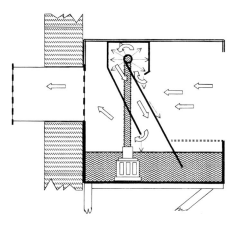

Above Spray Booth. A strong extractor fan is needed, with a sealed motor which will not be damaged by any dampness penetrating the filter. A guard should be fitted which prevents anyone harming themselves on the fan blades. A simple plywood box is mounted on the wall to contain any overspray.

Above, right Wet Back Spray Booth. In a wet back spray booth the overspray is drawn

through a series of water curtains which carry the glaze away to the reservoir below, where it settles out. This sediment can be cleaned out periodically. The main construction should be of sheet metal or glass fibre with a removable plug to drain away the sediment. The water is circulated by a submersible pump, through plastic piping to a horizontal tube which is drilled to produce a spray effect. A water-resistant fan should be fitted, preferably one with an externally mounted motor, as some water spray may be drawn through the system.

booth with an extractor fan, which sucks the dust into a filter, or in a water curtain spray booth, where droplets of glaze are caught by the water and carried away to a settling tank. It is possible to construct a spray booth with a filter which is both safe for the operator and for the environment. A simple construction from plywood will restrict the spread of glaze mist and allow the extractor fan to be more efficient.

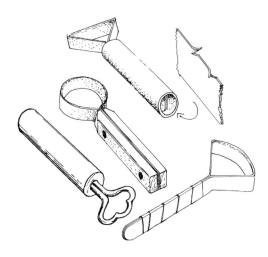

Hand tools

Tools are available from potters' suppliers but the advantage of custom-made equipment is obvious. They can be tailor-made to suit the individual requirements of the user, work well, and are often stronger and cheaper. By making specialised tools the potter extends his craftsmanship and his ability to make good craft products.

Modelling tools
Wood is a popular material with which to make modelling tools. It is pleasant to hold and can be reasonably easy to shape. Some softwoods can be easily abraded by clay and quickly lose their edge. Bamboo gives a sharp edge and can be used to cut clay. Another fine, hard-wearing, stable material is boxwood, often used to make tools and rulers.

Plastic and aluminium sheet can also be formed into modelling tools but it is worth looking at found objects such as old paintbrushes and knitting needles to see if they can be adapted for use.

Turning tools and knives
Turning tools are easily made from the thin metal strip used for binding wooden packing crates. The metal is usually

Strip tools and turning tools. The type of metal banding used to secure packing cases or bundles of timber in a builders merchant yard makes excellent material for turning tools. They can be bent to any shape and fitted with a handle if required using more scraps such as plastic water pipe, hose or even insulation tape. Sharpen the edge before use. An alternative to extruded handles can be found with wire cutters. The wire is bent into the desired profile and fitted with a strong handle, needed to drag the wire through a block of clay.

thrown away but it often has a rust-resistant coating and is a very useful material for the potter. A variety of useful shapes for turning tools can be fashioned in a few minutes using a pair of pliers and sheet metal shears or a hacksaw. The ends can be kept together and made safe by pushing on a piece of plastic water pipe or by binding with plastic tape to form a handle. Lastly, use a file to sharpen the cutting edge – it will stay sharp for a long time due to the thinness of the metal.

Another good source of metal for tools is worn-out hacksaw blades, particularly the industrial type, which are about 1.2 in. (30 mm) wide. As these blades are made from very hard carbon steel they must be heated to a red heat in order to bend them, or they will shatter. If a turning tool is needed, the saw teeth can first be ground off with a grinder to provide a cutting edge. The thin blades can then be bent into a loop style turning tool, or the wider blade will be thick enough to make a single strip tool with a cutting edge bent at right angles to the handle.

Cutting knives and scrapers can also be made from these blades and will last a long time. It is well worth spending some time making a comfortable handle for all of these tools, as this will improve control and safety when in use. A little imagination and a visit to the scrap bins will provide the ideal material, whether it be plastic piping, bamboo, wood, metal extrusions or some other suitable article.

Cutting wires and harps

There are many sources of wire suitable for cutting wires. If a fine wire is preferred then it is worth trying fishing tackle shops for plastic-coated, braided, stainless steel fishing-leader wire. Large steel washers or strips of wood are used as handles and when the wire is fixed firmly and the ends twisted around to avoid sharp points, the plastic cover can be burned off with a lighted match. If the cover is lit in the middle, the flames will burn down towards each end where they can be blown out, and the melted plastic will seal the frayed wire. Old guitar strings can be used, or single strand stainless wire can be purchased in bulk. This can either be used singly or doubled by joining two ends, gripping them in a vice, and fixing the other ends in a hand drill. By turning the drill handle slowly and maintaining slight pressure, useful lengths of twisted wire can be produced. This stronger wire

would be good for wedging or for making textured marks in the clay or the distinctive 'shell' pattern on the base of pots cut from the wheel.

Cutting slabs

Flat sheets of clay can be cut quickly and accurately from a block of clay by using a cutting wire. One method is to use two sticks with notches cut at regular intervals with a saw. The required thickness is selected on each stick and a cutting wire slotted in and held in place by hand. The wire should be kept tight when pulled through the block and the wire not allowed to sag. When the block of clay is lifted away, a slab of the desired thickness is exposed.

An alternative technique involves the use of a cutting harp. This can be simply made from a 35 in. (90 cm) length of 0.5 in. (15 mm) steel rod bent in to shape by clamping one end firmly in a vice, leaving about 7.8 in. (20 cm) of rod exposed. By slipping a 39 in. (1 m) length of 1 in. (2.54 cm) steel pipe over the end, the rod can be pulled into a right-angled position. The same process is applied to the other end, then a 2 mm hole is drilled 0.2 in. (5 mm) from each end of the rod. To tense up the wire, fix one end and pass the other end through the second hole. While a helper applies pressure on the steel rod to flex it slightly, secure the second end of the wire. When the pressure is released the wire will be stretched taut.

The clay block is placed on a flat surface and the harp wire is drawn through. The thickness is varied by raising the wire. Textured effects can be achieved by using different wires such as curtain wire or even old kiln elements that give a deep-ridged pattern.

When joining slabs of clay it is sometimes necessary to make an angled

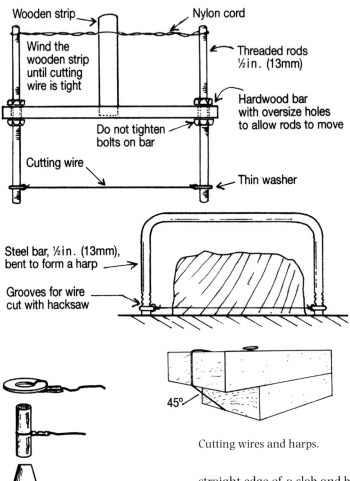

Cutting wires and harps.

cut or bevel along the edges of the clay so that the two surfaces form a mitre when they are put together. A simple tool which makes this job a lot easier is made from two pieces of wooden batten which are fixed together so that they overlap. The piece of wood on top should overlap the bottom piece by the thickness of the batten, forming an overhang which is as high as it is deep. When a piece of single strand wire is stretched across this gap it will form a 45° angle. The tool is placed against the

straight edge of a slab and by moving it sideways will cut a perfect bevel. Tools can also be made to accommodate other angles.

Rolling boards

When very regular, even rolled coils are needed for the production of handles or other details it is often difficult to make rolls of a consistent thickness. Yasuda's rolling board is a great help. A 11.8 x 15.7 in. (30 x 40 cm) plywood board is drilled at each corner to accept a 0.2 in. (5 mm) bolt. Each bolt is passed through the board and has two nuts on it, one on either side of the board so that it can be

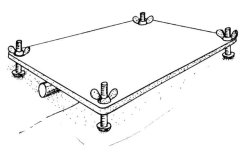

Coil Rolling Board. This design is used by Takeshi Yasuda to produce handles and attachments for his work. Thickness can be adjusted by screwing the bolts up or down. Coils can be textured by rolling on different surfaces.

Geoff Fuller makes his own brushes to help with particular stages of decoration. Bristles can be made from combinations of found materials.

locked in place. The bolt is adjusted so that the distance between the head of the bolt and the board is equal to the desired thickness of coil. Prepare a rough coil of clay by hand-rolling, and pinch the ends to prevent them becoming hollow. Give the coil a twist and then place under the rolling board which is rolled back and forth gently. Perfect coils of even thickness can be manufactured each time. An added bonus is that textured coils can be produced by rolling on to surfaces such as perforated metal sheet or coarse fabric.

Brushes

Geoff Fuller makes his own brushes for applying layers of slip. Each is produced individually to make a particular type of mark and to play its part in the making of his work. Simple wooden handles are fashioned, and bristles can be made from any suitable material such as hair, feathers, foam rubber or fibre from rope. Coarse materials can be bound directly to the handle with fine wire whilst finer fibres can be bundled together, dipped in glue and then set into a handle with a

drilled recess. By using a series of these bundles extra wide brushes can be made.

Slip trailers

Fine control of the flow of slip is essential when slip trailing, and this can be made more difficult when using the type of hard rubber bulb often used in college pottery departments. A good alternative can be made quite easily from a short length of bicycle inner tube, a rubber bung as used in wine making jars, a bulldog clip and an assortment of old pens. The inner tube is cut to about 7.9 in. (20 cm) long and wired on to the rubber bung with thin wire. The ball pens are dismantled and one plastic barrel selected, which is a good push fit into the bung. Slip is poured into the tube from a small jug and the end of the tube turned over a couple of times and then fastened with the bulldog clip. In use the trailer will respond to slight pressure and will not

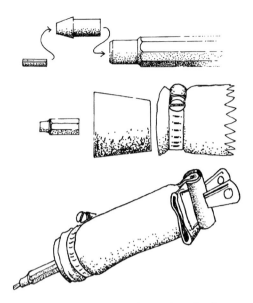

A good slip trailer made from a length of bicycle inner tube, a strong bulldog clip, a 'Jubilee' pipe clip and a variety of small pieces from ballpoint pens. The width of the 'trail' can be varied by changing the tip.

Tools for the wheel

Throwing ribs can be made from many different materials and each brings different qualities for working. Metal ribs can be smooth and thin, allowing fine control on smaller thrown pieces. By using a thin metal rib at right angles to the clay surface the thrower can produce a clean, flat finish to the clay without any throwing rings. To compress clay while throwing larger forms it may be necessary to use a thicker wooden rib. Some forms of plastic are easy to work with and can be used to make the type of rib used to add ridges or mouldings to thrown forms.

Although the abrasive nature of clay will eventually alter the shape of ribs made of soft materials such as aluminium, acrylic and wood, they can easily be replaced or reworked. Old credit cards can be used to try out ideas as they can be shaped in minutes using a craft knife, scissors and some fine sandpaper. Harder materials may need to be cut out with a jigsaw, bandsaw or metal cutting shears. Edges can be filed or sanded to a smooth finish.

Throwing guides are useful for repetition work. The simplest would be a ball of clay fixed to the rim of the wheel, with a wooden rod pushed into it and a feather fixed to the end which points to the top of the finished form. A more sophisticated adjustable model can be made from a slotted piece of wood and one or two pointers made from knitting needles that are held in place by butterfly bolts.

Callipers

Callipers are useful for measuring inside and outside forms and can be made from wood or plastic and a butterfly bolt. A double-ended calliper is useful if the

splutter and suck air back inside as the hard rubber trailers do. It can easily be washed out when a different colour is needed or, as the cost is minimal, several trailers can be made at once to keep a range of colours ready.

If the nozzle is too wide it can be narrowed down by using other parts of the ball pens. The brass fitting which holds the ink tube can be adapted by pulling off the tube, washing out the ink with detergent and finally removing the ball end with a pair of pliers. This should push back into the plastic barrel and draw very fine lines. Other nozzles can be made from the plastic ink tube or the plastic insulation found on electricity cables. If these are too narrow to fit the barrel they can be enlarged with a few turns of electrical insulation tape.

measurement has to be transferred from the inside of one form to the outside of another, as in the making of lids. The shape must be exactly symmetrical and the butterfly bolt will need to be at the halfway point if it is to be accurate. By moving the bolt away from the centre point it is possible to use the calliper to enlarge or reduce the measurement. Check the position needed for the fulcrum by opening one end of the pair of callipers to 4 in. (100 mm) and the other to, say, 4½ in. (115 mm) or equal to the shrinkage rate of your clay. When the correct position is found, the callipers will increase or decrease a measurement by the same percentage difference. This could be useful if allowances need to be made for clay shrinkage, for example, when calculating the size of a lid needed to fit a dry pot.

Roulettes

The potters at Whichford Pottery make their own decorating roulettes from biscuit clay and wire, to apply bands of decoration to their thrown forms. These are often made from clay, carved at the leatherhard stage and then biscuit fired and fitted with a simple wooden handle with a screw used as a spindle.

Scales and weighing

An item required by any potter who makes glazes or slips from recipes is a set of weighing scales. If small quantities of 100 g are required for tests, it will be necessary to weigh amounts of less than 1 g and to achieve this degree of accuracy usually requires expensive equipment such as the triple-beam balance – probably the best all-round scales for glaze mixing and testing. However, some domestic weighing scales

Whichford pottery: Roulettes

are reasonably accurate to 1 or 2 g, and it is possible to use these by weighing down to the smallest accurate amount and then pouring the material on to a piece of clean paper and dividing it up by eye. This method can produce reasonable results down to 0.25 g. If less accurate scales are to be used, beam balances are to be preferred as they will usually indicate how near the material is to a balance, whereas digital scales often have the habit of jumping between the two nearest numbers. Weights for balances can also be expensive, especially the smaller ones, but one alternative is to substitute another unit of weight. This could be something which is readily available, such as drawing pins or small nuts or bolts, which act as substitutes for the weights required by a test recipe. If a test is based on 60 g of one material and 40 g of another, the same ratios can be weighed using 60 drawing pins and 40 drawing pins or some other convenient unit.

When larger amounts need to be weighed for batch mixing of glazes, a lesser degree of accuracy is needed. Good results can be achieved from scales intended to be used in shops or kitchens, even if they are not large enough to hold bulky powdered materials. If some adjustment is possible for calibration this

Domestic scales and weights can often be accurate enough for weighing batches of glaze materials.

may allow a bowl or other container to be permanently used.

Those potters who mix their own clay bodies may need to weigh much larger quantities. Heavy duty spring-balances are useful for weighing bags of clay powder and they can be suspended from suitably strong ceiling joists, beams or door lintels. A canvas sling can be made to support paper sacks which have been opened. The type of scales used in the past by farmers to weigh sacks of vegetables would also be suitable if they turn up at farm auctions or junk shops.

Some materials used in clay bodies, such as sand or grog, can be measured quite accurately by volume, as they settle quickly when disturbed. A jug or other suitable container is filled with dry sand or grog, weighed, and a simple calculation made to tell how many jugs will be needed for the recipe. This method speeds up the measuring of sand and grog and could be used with other materials provided they are in exactly the same state of dryness and volume each time.

Safe workshop practice – equipment

- Even the simplest of hand tools can be a threat to your health and safety when misused. Knives or modelling tools, for example, may find their way into the reclaim bin with the scrap clay, presenting a potential hazard when the clay is scooped out by hand to be recycled.

- In most countries there are building regulations which limit the proximity of electrical sockets and water taps for safe use. The combination of water, wet clay and electrical equipment presents the risk of electric shock. Check that all electrical appliances are well insulated and maintained. Never have wet hands when using switches. Alternatively, have a qualified electrician fit sealed, waterproof switches to equipment such as wheels that are regularly used in wet conditions.

- Pugmills should be fitted with an approved switch which will cut off the machine when the hopper handle is lifted.

- Any equipment made by the potter must also conform to national safety standards as applied to industry. For example, home-made wheels which use a pulley system must also include suitable covers for the drive belts and electrical gear, dough mixers used to prepare clay should have an easily accessible cut-off switch. Avoid any compromises where safety is concerned and consider health and safety to be an essential part of good professional practice. In this way potters should be able to work in a safe environment.

Chapter Four
Kilns

These essential pieces of equipment need to be carefully selected. The performance and specifications of a kiln will apply many constraints on the potter's work, as no kiln is capable of the complete range of firing qualities available.

Fuel types

The type of fuel available is an important factor to be taken into consideration. Virtually any material that produces heat has been used to fire pots in the past, from animal dung to solar energy. Coal and coke have largely gone out of use as electricity, gas and oil have become widely available. Often a good source of cheap fuel will encourage inventiveness, and potters have developed techniques for using some of the less likely materials such as sawdust, waste oil, and heavy fuel oil.

Developments in modern hot-face insulation has meant that new kilns can be more efficient and cheaper to fire, but these materials tend to be soft and more prone to damage than the older high temperature insulation bricks. The cost of efficient insulation is also high although savings may be made in fuel.

Kiln building

Second-hand insulation and firebricks are often available for kiln building if you are prepared to search them out.

They may come from another potter who is dismantling a kiln, or another good source is companies who use heat treatment as part of their manufacturing process. Brickworks, iron and steel foundries, and other industries, use kilns and furnaces which are relined at regular intervals. As the bricks are often used without a permanent mortar, many of the old bricks are quite serviceable and may be available for a small price.

Bricks can be made by hand if a good source of raw material is available. Firebricks that are to be used on the hot face will need a suitable fireclay and if there is a supply available to you it may be worth carrying out some tests. Hot-face insulation can be made from a mixture of china clay and sawdust in equal parts, with enough water added to make a stiff mix, and pressed into wooden moulds. The bricks are dried and fired slowly to 1000°C (1832°F), during which the sawdust burns out, leaving a porous brick which is about 15% smaller, through shrinkage, than the original.

A castable mix can be made and the kiln can be built using wooden moulds and shuttering. For a high temperature kiln used for soda glazing, Jack Doherty has developed a mix, which can also be used for a conventional stoneware kiln.

A small amount of water is added and the ingredients stirred to a stiff mixture that will just hold together when squeezed. It can then be rammed into wooden formers, to produce a monolithic structure which is fired *in situ*, or into moulds producing sections which can be biscuit fired before building into an arch.

Fireclay	4
Sawdust	4 (fine sawdust and wood chippings)
Grog	4 (dust to 5 mm)
Cement	1
Alumina	1 (salt or soda kiln only)
(Parts by volume)	

A mix for low temperature firing at temperatures up to cone 02 (approximately 1100°C (2012°F) is:

Fine vermiculite	6
Fireclay	1
(Parts by volume)	

This should be mixed to a slightly wetter mix than the recipe above, and should push out through the fingers when squeezed in the hand. This softer mix is best used as a casting mix, shovelled into wooden moulds to form blocks which are then biscuit fired before assembling into a kiln.

A small kiln which is good for low temperature firings up to cone 02 can be made from the vermiculite casting mix listed above. A square mould is used, made from strips of wood 6 in. (15 cm) wide and up to 39 in. (1 m) long, depending on the size of kiln, which can range from 1 to 6 cu. ft. (28-150 l.). The mould is filled, with the mix firmly packed and the top suface scraped with a flat board. Each slab is cast and allowed to dry thoroughly before removing carefully from the mould. The slabs are very fragile at this stage. Four slabs should be cast in this way and then

fired to cone 04 (approximately 1050°C (1922°F)), leaving gaps between them to allow for heat circulation.

The floor is made from two layers of firebricks, on top of a layer of concrete blocks sitting on a concrete base. A 4 x 4 in. (10 x 10 cm) hole is cut for the burner and another 6in. (15 cm) diameter for the flue, using a padsaw or similar blade. The kiln is assembled from the fired panels and secured with 9 in. (25 cm) lengths of welding rod, pinning the panels together. The door is made by stacking insulation bricks in the opening. Additional firebrick buttresses can be placed around the kiln to improve stability.

This kiln must not be allowed to get wet as the vermiculite will begin to disintegrate. It should be built in a sheltered position outside or inside, with a hood and flue pipe to remove fumes. For the 1 cu. ft (28 l.) size, a large plumber's blowtorch will be sufficient to

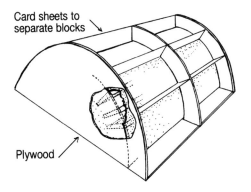

Card sheets to separate blocks

Plywood

Diagram of mould for kiln arch blocks. 3 mm thick, non-tempered hardboard is flexible enough to bend to the required shapes when dampened with water-soaked sheets of newspaper for a few hours. Sections are cast one at a time and when the whole arch is cast, it is dismantled, dried and biscuit fired. Allow for shrinkage when calculating the size of the fired arch.

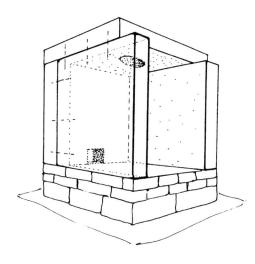

Low temperature cast vermiculite kiln. A square wooden mould is made and each slab is cast and allowed to dry thoroughly before removing carefully from the mould. The slabs are very fragile at this stage. Four slabs should be fired to cone 04 (approximately 1050°C (1922°F)), leaving gaps to allow for heat circulation. The floor is made from two layers of firebricks, on top of a layer of concrete blocks sitting on a concrete base. The kiln is assembled from the fired panels and secured with 9 in. (25 cm) lengths of welding rod. The door is made by stacking one layer of insulation bricks in the opening. Additional firebrick buttresses can be placed around the kiln to improve stability.

fire up to 1000°C (1832°F).

Building your own kiln allows you to tailor the structure to your own needs, allowing you to develop the technology most suitable for the production of particular types of work. For example Esias Bosch, a potter in White River, South Africa, has designed and made an unusual, 'flat' electric kiln to fire his enormous 97.5 x 49 in. (2.5 x 1.25 m) porcelain panels. Other potters continually make refinements and adjustments to the structure of their

kiln or successive kilns in order to improve firing qualities.

If you are considering buying a kiln, whether new or old, bear in mind the size of entrance doorways. Some kilns are designed to be small enough to go through a standard doorway and others are built on site, or made in sections, but many simply depend on sufficiently wide access being available

All kilns need to be sited in a dry area with good ventilation to cope with the fumes given off during firing, most prevalent during biscuit firings of sulphurous clay but also present in enamel and glaze firing. An extractor fan, fitted to a hood and suspended over the kiln, is the most effective way to remove kiln fumes and is necessary where the kiln is sited in a building used for other activities. Some manufacturers of electric kilns supply a venting system with extractor fan. When the kiln room is separate from other buildings, such as an outbuilding or garage, and the amount of time spent working in the room during firings is limited, sufficient ventilation can be obtained from open windows and doors. Further information on the safe siting of kilns can be found in this chapter's section on safe workshop practice.

Electricity

This can be a versatile means of heating a kiln, providing there is a ready supply nearby, as the cost of having a mains supply laid any distance is prohibitive. Temperatures up to 1300°C (2372°F) are possible with a neutral atmosphere, and although some experimental work has been carried out with reduction in electric kilns, this is often regarded as detrimental to the heating elements. However there are many potters in

Japan who regularly produce a reduction atmosphere in electric kilns, using small amounts of gas or other flammable material such as splinters of wood. This system provides reduction facilities in areas where fuel-burning kilns are prohibited.

It is possible to run modern kilns of 1.2 cu. ft. (27 *l.*) from a domestic 13 amp socket and up to about 4.3 cu. ft. (120 *l.*) wired into a domestic 30 amp circuit, but sizes greater than this will depend on the type of supply to the property and may use up to 100 amps for a 45 cu. ft. (1227 *l.*) model.

Temperature controllers can range from simple 'low, medium and high' switches to reasonably inexpensive microprocessor systems which can be programmed to govern the rate of increase in temperature, final temperature or soak, and even a controlled rate of cooling. This amount of regulation means that much if not all of the firing can be automated and can be timed to use cheap rate electricity, or just free the potter to carry out other activities.

Top-loading kilns are the least expensive to buy, mainly because they do not need the stronger structure required to support the hinged door of a front loader, and are therefore easier to construct. As each shelf is packed with pots, care must be taken to check the gap between the tallest pot and the shelf above. This is best done by resting a straight surface between the shelf props when the pots are in place. Front-loading kilns have the advantage of being slightly easier to pack as the clearance between pots and shelf can be checked visually.

Second-hand electric kilns may be a good alternative, depending on their previous treatment. Look for cracks, chips missing from the brickwork, and evidence of glaze melted into the surface, all of which will reduce the kiln's efficiency, and may indicate over-firing or heavy usage. If the coils of the elements are lying flat or bulge out of their supports they may be due for replacement and it could prove costly to replace a complete set. Look out for signs of rust in the steel framework, caused by condensation trying to escape during the firing.

It is quite feasible to build your own electric kiln. The subject should be thoroughly researched, of course, and all work must be checked by a qualified electrician before connection.

Electric kiln

Design by Richard Godfrey

The simple structure meant that it was relatively straightforward to build. A sheet of stainless steel sheet forms the casing, which is lined with bricks and backed with ceramic fibre. The case is then tightened onto the bricks with adjusting screws. Some people are put off by the calculations needed to ensure

Richard Godfrey's Electric Kiln. Richard Godfrey cut grooves into the insulation bricks to hold the elements and calculated the angles needed to complete the oval shape. The lid is lifted clear of the kiln for packing and unpacking.

the correct element size and even heating. Richard based his calculations on a commercial kiln and then checked with an element supplier before placing his order. The elements are supported in grooves cut into lightweight insulation bricks with a tubular Surform file. The lid is built from insulation bricks, bonded together with high temperature cement and bound with a stainless steel strip. It is lifted on and off the kiln each time it is fired.

The kiln is used for twice-weekly production firings and has proved to be reliable, with consistently even temperatures. One modification may be the use of ceramic fibre in the lid to make it lighter.

Gas

It is possible to produce all types of ceramic work in a gas kiln. Oxidised and reduced atmospheres are possible along with low and high temperature firings, the maximum temperature limited only by the construction and materials used. Gas burners are designed for mains supply or bottled gas, butane or propane, and are not interchangeable. In some cases they can be recalibrated by

changing the gas jet and this should be carried out by a qualified gas fitter. The air supply to the flame will either rely on 'natural draught' or on an electric fan.

Many potters fire kilns using very basic power controls, with a gas valve to increase the heat, along with a flame failure control which will cut off the gas if the flame goes out. This protects against the danger of potentially explosive unburned gas and air building up in the kiln chamber. Simple but efficient gas burners can be manufactured from pipe fittings.

Electronic automatic temperature and atmospheric controls are available, but at present seem to be more successful on the larger-scale industrial kilns.

With all fuels that produce flames, a flue is required to take away the waste gases and this may be a problem in some buildings. Updraught kilns do not rely on the flue to pull air through the chamber and an air gap can be included, above the kiln, which will allow cool air to mix with the hot kiln gases. Downdraught kilns do rely on a good

Propane Gas system. A typical piping system for a small kiln.

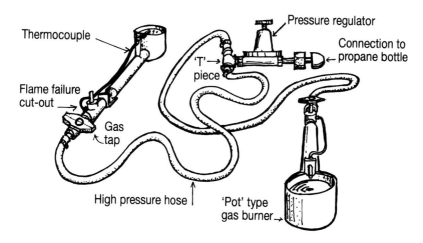

47

draught and the flue should run vertically from the kiln with as little horizontal run as possible. Care should be taken where the flue passes through a ceiling or roof, to ensure that there is sufficient insulation or air-gap between the hot flue and any combustible material, to prevent fire. There will be building regulations which govern this.

An inexpensive gas kiln

Design by students of the Royal Forest of Dean College, Gloucestershire
Students at the Royal Forest of Dean College, looking for an economical way to make a gas kiln, converted an old electric kiln into a gas kiln. The original frame, casing and brickwork were in a reasonable condition and were left intact when the elements were stripped out. A flue was constructed on to the back, in the space which had held the electrical connections. Two burner ports were

drilled through the floor, using a simple cutter made from a piece of 3 in. (7.5 cm) pipe with teeth cut into the end. Two 'pot'-type propane burners were mounted underneath. As the kiln was to be used for vapour glazing, the inside was coated with a refractory wash which, to some extent, protects the insulation bricks from the corrosive soda vapour.

The kiln is fired regularly to 1280°C (2336°F), and will achieve top temperature in six hours.

Gas trolley kiln

Design by Simon Hulbert
As a maker of large, individual pieces and smaller garden pots, Simon Hulbert needed a kiln which was easy to pack and fire. This kiln is designed so that the hearth can be rolled out of the kiln during packing and unpacking, providing access from three sides. A seal is made between the two parts by the use of grog-filled steel channel fitted to the kiln, which engages with a length of angle iron fitted to the trolley. The door is bricked up before each firing. Firings take over two or three days, in order to ensure thorough drying before the temperature rises, and to protect the large forms from thermal shock.

Raku kiln

Design by Ian Byers
A functional raku kiln can be made very quickly with the simplest of materials. Ian Byers has developed this kiln using pottery techniques. It is almost a pot-shaped kiln, made from a mixture of clay and aggregate, formed into coils

Gas kiln conversion using a disused electric kiln.

Top Simon Hulbert's trolley kiln. High temperature insulation bricks are backed up by a lower grade insulation on the outside. The trolley hearth allows excellent access to pack the larger pots.

Above Ian Byer's raku kiln. Constructed using pottery techniques, this kiln can be made quickly, and functions well as a raku kiln fired to around 1000°C.

which are built up from a flat base at a thickness of about 3.1 in. (8 cm). As the kiln does not need to go much above 900°C, the clay can be of any type available. The aggregate can either be crushed insulation brick or, preferably, the expanded clay pellets produced as a soilless medium for large pot plants. The size of the kiln is only limited by the making technique, but a reasonable height would be around 20-23 in. (50-60 cm). Two 28,000 Btu standard blowtorch burners should be sufficient for this size of kiln. The openings for these, made either with a large kiln prop or from a card tube which will burn away in firing, are positioned through the wall at an angle to the chamber to allow the flame to circulate. A large door opening at the front, and a smaller flue at the top, both give access for loading and removing raku pots. The door itself can be made from insulation bricks bound together with wire, and a broken kiln shelf used to control the flue. This kiln can be built in a few hours, heated with a small fire, allowed to dry overnight, and fired the next day. It reaches temperature quickly and holds the heat well between unpacking of fired pots and the loading of the next batch. The heat does not fire the kiln wall throughout and consequently is not weatherproof.

Oil

The most commonly used heating oils are diesel (domestic heating oil, or gas oil) and kerosene. Commercially produced burners are available for oil although many potters prefer to make their own.

The simplest system for burning oil consists of sloping metal plates arranged in the firebox as a series of steps. A small

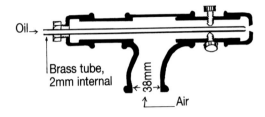

Oil burner pipe fittings. An efficient oil burner can be made from pipe fittings, with an air supply provided by the exhaust from a tube-type vacuum cleaner.

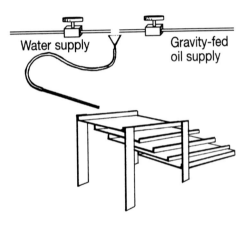

Drip feed oil burner. A good system for burning waste oil is the stepladder burner. A minimum of three steel steps are arranged at the mouth of the firebox, either welded in place or propped on brick supports. A small fire is started in front of the burner and oil is dripped on the top plate. As the firebox warms up, the oil burns from higher steps and the burner becomes more efficient. Water can be dripped with the oil and has the effect of spreading the flame. No electricity is needed but the kiln needs to have a good draught.

fire or blowtorch is initially applied to the bottom shelf and the oil is dripped onto the top metal plate. As the heat builds up, the draught will increase and pull more air through the 'burner', making it work more efficiently.

Slightly more sophisticated burners, again simple to construct, can be made from pipe fittings. The outlet from a vacuum cleaner can deliver an inexpensive supply of compressed air, required by this burner to vaporise the oil. The oil needs to be supplied under pressure and so the storage tank must be raised at least 4–8 ft. (1.2–2.4 m) above the burner.

Both of these burners have the added advantage that they can burn waste oil such as used engine oil. This cheap source of fuel contains minute amounts of metals and fluxes that can act as a vapour glaze, adding flashes of warm colour to pots in the kiln.

Oil-fired salt kiln

Design by Richard Dewar

This 70 cu. ft. (2000 l.) kiln is used for salt glazing. The walls are constructed of heavy firebricks and the roof is made from lightweight insulation brick. Steel tie bars prevent the sprung arch from flattening out. A simple alternative to a hinged door is provided by a door (wicket) which is rebuilt with loose bricks each firing. The two industrial burners use compressed air to vaporise kerosene oil just inside the fireboxes. Salt is introduced into the fireboxes from 1200°C, using a length of angle iron to tip it in. Carborundum shelving is used to withstand the effect of the corrosive salt vapour, and wads of china clay and alumina prevent the pots from sticking to the shelves.

Wood

When used as a fuel, wood can become another tool of the potter, who can use the effect of the flame to decorate and

Oil-fired salt kiln after firing.
Photo: Richard Dewar

enrich the surface of his work.

Part of the process of wood firing is ensuring a supply of good seasoned wood. To release the maximum amount of heat in the firebox, wood needs to be as dry as possible. This means that the 'wood firer' has to have enough sheltered space to store timber while it dries, or alternatively is able to secure a good supply of kiln-ready firewood. The initial slow drying out occurs as the 'sap' moisture leaves the wood. If the wood is subsequently wetted by rain etc., it will be much easier to dry again.

A well-designed and fired wood kiln can be very efficient and is a good choice in areas where other fuels are scarce. It also utilises a renewable source of energy, often in the form of scrap off-cuts of other processes that would otherwise be wasted.

Through-draught wood kiln

This is an efficient design for a kiln fired by wood, which can be easily fired to earthenware temperatures when built with inexpensive materials such as house bricks. When used for raku firing, this kiln is capable of reaching temperature very quickly if good dry wood is used. For higher temperatures, better insulation will be needed in the shape of high-temperature insulation bricks for the chamber, and a good quality firebrick for the firebox.

The basic design uses kiln shelves to span both the firebox and chamber, and these will probably be one of the biggest expenses. This kiln has a packing area of about 1 cu. ft. (28 *l*.), although by building an arch over the firebox, larger sizes up to 15 cu. ft. (420 *l*.) can be constructed. As the size of the chamber is increased, the firebox must be scaled up to the same proportion in order to maintain adequate heat input. A larger version of the kiln, with two opposing fireboxes, is used by many potters and is mentioned in *The Kiln Book* by F. Olsen. The design is often called the 'fast-fire' kiln and it has been shown to fire to stoneware temperatures in well under five hours.

The effect of the wood firing on the work in this type of kiln is not as pronounced as it would be in some other kilns. The flame sometimes produces flashes of warm colour, and deposits of ash blowing through the kiln produce glaze on unglazed areas of pots, and enrich applied glazes.

Straight from the kiln – wood-fired pots by Jack Troy showing flashing effects. Photo: Jack Doherty

Basic wood fired kiln. When used for raku firing at about 1000°C (1832°F) this kiln may be constructed from common clay house bricks. Higher temperatures can be achieved with refractory bricks and improved insulation.

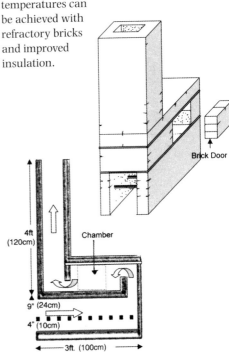

Brick Door

4ft (120cm)

Chamber

9" (24cm)

4" (10cm)

3ft. (100cm)

Anagama kiln

Design by Jack Troy

Jack Troy uses his anagama kiln to enrich the surface of his pottery, as the flame moves through the kiln, carrying the wood ash that settles on his work. The long boat-shaped kiln holds pots that represent many weeks work. Packing and firing the kiln is also a long process. Jack's work is placed in the kiln unglazed and he relies entirely on the firing to produce colour and texture on the surface of his pots. The kiln is kept at a high temperature for many hours, allowing the ash to build up on the surface of the pieces, and combine with other fluxes to form colour and glaze. The four-day firing means that a team of helpers are needed to stoke the fireboxes at regular intervals and keep the temperature rising.

Safe workshop practice – kilns

- A kiln room, or outside kiln area, is preferable, as all types of kiln firings have the potential of producing toxic gases. Chlorine, fluorine, sulphur dioxide and ozone can all be produced during firings. Biscuit firings can produce sulphur dioxide from particular clays, carbon monoxide from fuel-burning kilns and metal fumes (including lead) from high-temperature firings. Although most fumes will be taken away through the flue of a fuel-burning kiln, good ventilation is important for all kilns, including electric kilns, in enclosed spaces. If the kiln is in a work area this may be in the form of a canopy hood fitted either to a chimney or extractor fan to take the fumes outside the building. When the kiln is

Inside Jack Troy's anagama kiln. The pots are stacked directly on the hearth and sometimes stacked up on top of each other. Varied colour and textural effects are created by the long firing and the passage of flames and wood ash through the chamber. Photo: Jack Doherty

in a separate room, then a simple extractor will be sufficient. Whenever an extractor fan is fitted, allowance should be made for fresh air to enter the room through a suitable vent in a door or wall. A carbon monoxide detector should be fitted where a fuel-burning kiln is operated indoors.
- Heat given off from the kiln will often raise the temperature of the workshop to an excessive level, making an unpleasant working environment and drying out work too quickly.
- Suitable protective shoes and clothing should be worn when firing the kiln.

Long hair, medallions and even long beards can be dangerous.

- The red to yellow glow of a hot kiln gives off infra-red radiation and eye protection must be worn when looking into the kiln. Infra-red goggles to an approved standard are available. Alternatively welder's goggles or a hand-held shield can be used. Dark, green glass lenses reduce the amount of infra-red light.

- All combustible and flammable materials should be stored well away from kiln areas and kilns sited at least 23 in. (60 cm) away from walls. A similar gap should be left under the kiln to allow air to circulate, and the kiln should be placed on a fireproof surface. Where a flue passes through a ceiling or wall, precautions must be taken to insulate the flue from combustible materials, and to include weatherproof flashing outside to prevent rainwater finding its way into the workshop. Local building regulations will give detailed requirements.

- Propane gas is heavier than air and good ventilation should be provided at ground level if the kiln is sited indoors.

- Ceramic fibre is a very efficient insulator and has been used in the construction of many kilns. Recent studies have given rise to concerns over its effect on health. Check with the current health and safety regulations for its use and follow them closely.

- Consideration must be given to the floor loading when deciding on the siting of kilns, particularly in the case of larger sizes such as a 13 cu. ft.

(64 *l.*) kiln will weigh about 1 tonne (1000 kg). Kilns built *in situ* should have a solid concrete base sufficiently thick to take the weight of the kiln and at least two layers of firebrick (to prevent the heat reaching the concrete which may explode with catastrophic results). The total weight of a kiln that is made from firebrick is colossal – 250 bricks weigh about 1 tonne. If in any doubt, it is best to take advice from local authorities about the safe siting of your kiln and use qualified personnel to connect, or at least inspect, electricity and gas supplies.

- All kilns, whether flame or electric, should be serviced on a regular basis, depending on the amount of usage. Checks should be made on electrical insulation and connections, safety cut-off switches, burner jets, condition of flues and the kiln structure.

- Noise produced by compressors, blowers, or the burners themselves can be a hazard, particularly over a long period.

- Specialised types of kilns such as raku, salt-glaze and wood-firing kilns are best sited on an outdoor kiln site, preferably away from other buildings so that the smoke and fumes are not a nuisance to others. Precautions should also be taken by the kiln operators to avoid breathing fumes emitted by them. If the site is accessible to the general public, steps should be taken to protect them from the dangers of hot kilns which may be left unattended at the end of a firing.

Chapter Five
Business

Although the success of a pottery business depends on a combination of many factors, the most important element is the work itself. The business administration, promotion and marketing must all be directed to support the quality and style of your work, which should be produced as economically and efficiently as possible without compromising the particular features which provide its individuality and character.

Two people who can offer good advice on the starting up of a business are a solicitor, who can tell you about legal requirements, and an accountant who can give guidance on how the business records should be kept.

Business plan

This is a valuable way of finding out what you will need to start your business, and will be a useful guide in the early stages. Banks and other funding bodies will expect to see one if you want to borrow money from them and it will form part of any application for setting up grants or loans.

Clear objectives should be described in the business plan. Even if a potter is working alone it is important that clear objectives are set so that the success of

the workshop can be properly assessed. In the case of two or more people working together in a partnership, it is essential that objectives are agreed at the outset. Short-term objectives may include securing adequate funding to establish the workshop and generating sufficient turnover to provide a living wage and make a profit. Long-term

Good marketing material brings your work to the attention of potential customers.

objectives may include: gaining recognition from a professional body; continuing to develop a personal style; exhibiting internationally; and ensuring the business continues to expand, etc. These objectives should also reflect the constraints imposed on the business by outside forces, including planning laws, taxes, health and safety laws.

Other important elements to include in a business plan are cash-flow forecast, details about yourself and your work, curriculum vitae, market research, details of equipment and other resources already acquired, equipment, materials needed, how much you need to borrow and why.

The cash flow forecast shows how you expect your business to run, usually over a period of a year. Estimates of income and expenditure are included, based on as much factual evidence as possible. A good plan will include results of market research, costs of production, repayment of any loans and other expenses, when sales may be expected and why. It should be as realistic as possible and at the same time show that your project is viable. The example below shows a cash flow for four months.

Finance

Capital will be required in order to set up a business. If you do not already own a property then you will need to rent or raise a mortgage to buy. Equipment, materials, tools and promotional material will be needed, and you will need to support yourself until the first sales begin to return some cash. There may be some sources of funding available to help with this start-up stage. A suitably prepared business plan is

CASH FLOW	April	May	June	July
Income				
Sales	650	750	1150	1650
Grants	180	180	180	180
Loans	1000			
Total Income	**1830**	**930**	**1330**	**1830**
Expenditure				
Rent	208	208	208	208
Fuel	80	80	30	0
Telephone	0	50	0	0
Materials	350	90	100	0
Tools	0	20	0	0
Car Expenses	0	150	150	120
Cash Drawings	400	400	400	400
Repayments	300	300	300	300
Equipment	400	40	0	0
Total Expenditure	**1738**	**1338**	**1188**	**1028**
(Net loss)/Net profit per month	**92**	**-408**	**142**	**802**
Cumulative (loss)/profit	**92**	**-316**	**-174**	**648**

likely to be an important part of any application. In the United Kingdom there are organisations such as The Training and Enterprise Council (TEC), The Crafts' Council Setting-Up Grant and The Prince's Youth Business Trust which administer grants, loans and other assistance to people starting a new business. There may be other schemes relevant to your locality and it would be worthwhile finding out what support is available.

If there are no grants or low interest loans available and capital is not forthcoming from any other source, it will be necessary to approach a bank for a loan to start the business. You will need to show the bank your business plan to demonstrate that your proposed business is a good investment and has a chance of success. The repayment of any loan will be included in the plan.

Costing your work

Before any profit can be made from selling ceramics the true production cost must be worked out. Once this figure is established, it is possible to estimate a selling price which will include an element of profit. The production costs will be the sum of the business overheads and your labour.

Overheads

When calculating the total cost of producing a particular item there are certain costs which must be taken into consideration before any clay work begins. These are the workshop overheads which include all of the expenses excepting labour. Include everything which is needed in order for your enterprise to function. An example of the overheads for an individual working in a small fictitious workshop is shown.

Workshop overheads for One Year

Rent or repayments for workshop	£2500
Gas and electricity	700
Maintenance and repairs	250
Consumables	80
Car expenses	1660
Telephone	375
Advertising and promotion	250
Insurance	265
Postage, stationery and carrier charges	350
Stock and raw materials	560
Equipment	250
Accountant	200
Total	**£7440**

To calculate the weekly cost of overheads, divide the annual costs by the number of working weeks: £7440 divided by 48 weeks is £155 per week.

An hourly rate is calculated by dividing the weekly rate by the number of hours spent making. Even though you may be working for 40 hours each week, for a single potter, the actual time spent making pots may only be a fraction of this. The remaining time will be spent on tasks other than production, such as ordering materials, answering telephone enquiries, etc. If 40% of the week is spent on other tasks, then only 24 hours is actual making time.

If you divide the £155 per week overhead rate by the 24 hours actual working time, then the hourly overhead rate is £6.46 per hour. The overheads will form part of the cost of whatever you make.

Labour Costs

Another factor to take into consideration is the cost of your labour. This is usually a high proportion of the costs, as most ceramic work is 'labour intensive', particularly if you are just starting out. You should consider whether you could speed up production as this will have a direct effect on the cost of the work. It will be necessary to work out an hourly rate for your time, based on your living costs and how much you expect to get from your business. Take the amount that you expect to earn in one year and calculate an hourly rate for your labour costs. If, for example, you need to take £10,000 per year in earnings, then divide this by the number of weeks worked in the year – £10,000 divided by 48 weeks is £208.30 per week. If your actual production time is 24 hours then the hourly rate will be £208.30 divided by 24 which is £8.68 per hour.

It is a valuable exercise to record the actual time it takes to make an object. Include all stages of production, even the moving of work to facilitate drying, and packing the kiln. If the work is produced in batches then record the total time taken and divide this by the number of pieces in the batch to find the time taken to make one.

Material costs
Calculate the cost of materials used for a range of different products. This should include the cost of clay, glazes, and other ceramic materials and should include delivery and items such as packaging materials. It should be possible to work out an average cost of materials per kilogram.

Firing costs
The cost of firing can be calculated by investigating the actual cost of fuel used in a firing and dividing this by the average number of pieces of work per firing, which will give a rough cost per pot. Firing costs are reduced when the kiln is fully packed, with no wasted space. In a small kiln it may be worth considering how many pieces can be placed on each shelf, as small adjustments to the size of work can often mean that you can get more into each firing. Once calculated, the fuel costs can be included in the workshop overheads and added into the hourly overhead rate.

Contingency
A contingency figure is an additional sum which should be added to the total cost to cover any unexpected expenses such as breakage or increased material costs. This 10–20% can be considered as additional profit if not actually required as a contingency. The amount may also reflect the reliability of the chosen production process. A potter who makes repetition earthenware in an electric kiln with an electronic controller may have a higher success rate than a potter who makes individual salt-glazed pieces fired with wood.

All of the above information can be used to establish the cost of making a pot. The following example shows the final calculation for costing a decorative teapot.

Labour	1.5 hours @ £8.68	13.02
Overhead	1.5 hours @ £6.46	9.69
Materials		2.50
Making price		**25.21**
Contingency of 10%		2.53
Cost of one teapot		**27.74**

This process will give a base figure and, if all expenses have been included, you will not make a loss if the item were sold at this price. There is no room to offer any discount as this figure represents the true cost. If the piece is to be sold on to a gallery or craft shop, this could be looked on as the wholesale price. The shop or gallery owner will add on their own costs, based on their overheads and working hours, to arrive at their retail price.

Other methods of costing work

You may find that your work sells well and the actual selling price may be much higher than the cost price. You will be following consumer demand, a process known as demand pricing, which requires a knowledge of the customer, the market and the competition, which is never easy for the small business person. Basically, the objective is to find out how much an article is worth and then see if you can produce it profitably. This would also apply if work is carried out for a commission with a fixed budget. Of course an understanding of the cost of production is still vital.

In the creative world of ceramics where individuality is valued, it is difficult to compare prices of different products. Visits to craft shops, galleries, potters' markets, etc. will give a good idea of the range of prices asked by a variety of makers, but the biggest dilemma will be how to compare work of varying styles made by different individuals. These prices will reflect the quality of the work, the popularity or status of the maker, and the success of the outlet or the maker in attracting customers.

With one-off or individual sculptural pieces the process of pricing work is even more complex. A basic costing will form a starting point but this will not necessarily reflect the success of the piece as an art object. This can only be judged by the maker and customer on a piece by piece basis. Some people prefer to use a formula where they take the

height plus the width of a sculpture and multiply this by a price per centimetre. A system like this can be applied to a variety of forms and gives some consistency. It also allows for simple increases and decreases of prices on a percentage basis when they need to be adjusted for retail selling or discounting.

Whatever system is adopted for pricing your work, the true cost price should form the basis of any calculations. Some small crafts businesses produce a very low income, generated by extremely long working hours which can be damaging to health, lifestyle and relationships. This may be because they have not costed their time properly, they are not working efficiently or their overheads are too high. Where possible work to enjoy life.

Business analysis

A simple business analysis called SWOT, useful for identifying Strengths, Weaknesses, Opportunities and Threats, can be applied both to your whole plan for starting a business and also to individual components such as marketing, or skills and ideas.

An analysis of a plan for starting a pottery business, for example, may comment on:

- Strengths: General economic conditions; location of the business; your own creative ability; lateral thinking; multi-skills; previous experience; anticipated commissioned work, etc.
- Weaknesses: Lack of business experience; lack of marketing information; manufacturing problems; lack of capital, etc.
- Opportunities: Improvement in personal circumstances; availability of suitable property; increase in

interest in craft pottery. Many a good idea is lost by not being able to recall it later, so record them in a notebook.

- Threats: Competition; increased borrowing rates/rent; recession; negative aspects from external environment in general.

Legal restrictions – planning regulations

Most workshops will come under some kind of local planning regulations. These are usually designed to control the development of buildings including houses and commercial premises. Check to find out if there are planning regulations which may affect your proposed pottery workshop. Separate permission may be needed if you intend to sell from the premises.

Ideally look for buildings with existing planning permission or established use. If an application has to be made for planning consent, make sure that full details are provided, but be careful in the choice of words when describing the nature of your work. Discuss your needs with the local planning authority before submitting an application. Pottery workshops are often classified as 'light industry' and are grouped with other 'industrial' processes, yet your proposal may be for a small, one-person workshop which would have far less impact on the local area.

Types of business

Businesses are recognised in most countries as belonging to particular categories. If a potter is self-employed in the United Kingdom he is known as a 'sole trader'. This is the simplest form of business with few requirements imposed, but it does have disadvantages. There is no distinction made between private and business finances and if you are unlucky enough to go broke, your personal possessions may be seized by the creditors. It is advisable to run separate bank accounts for your personal and business finances, to avoid confusion.

To avoid the risk of losing your possessions to a creditor it may be possible to form a limited company. This would mean that your liability will be limited to the value of your shareholding in the company, which is usually kept to a reasonably low figure. This is not normally relevant for most pottery businesses in the early stages. There are costs involved in setting up a limited company and you will also be required to provide much more financial information on a regular basis. As the person running the company you will be the director.

A partnership is a formal arrangement where two or more people share the running of the business. A partner may be considered because of their ability to help with a heavy workload (it may also be possible to hire extra help instead) or to bring in more capital or other expertise needed by the business. Seek advice from your accountant before entering into this type of arrangement. It is always advisable to get a clear agreement drawn up by a solicitor before entering into a partnership so that all participants agree on their responsibilities and their share of the business, profits or debts.

Taxation

There are many different types of taxation and it would be impossible to set out any specific guidelines. Most tax agencies have advisors and will supply information if contacted directly. Copies of useful and free leaflets are available in the United Kingdom from the Inland Revenue. The rules are quite different regarding the taxation of companies and the taxation of individuals.

Health and safety

Most countries have legislation regarding health and safety, although they will vary depending on your location. These issues affect the potter in several ways. Pots must be safe for the customer to use and must satisfy any standards laid down in law. Safe workshop practices must be in place to ensure the safety of employees, customers and the environment.

Contracts

Work which is carried out to order should be covered by some form of contract. The details will vary but generally this should include an agreement on what the work will be like, terms of payment, who pays for delivery and delivery dates (whether binding or not) and if installation is involved, who will do it and who will pay for it. Seek professional advice from a solicitor.

Copyright

Copyright laws are intended to protect original artistic, literary, dramatic and musical work against reproduction by others without permission of the maker. Whether a particular piece of work comes under the protection of copyright can only be determined through the courts; however, there is nothing to prevent makers from using the international © symbol followed by their name and the year in order to indicate that copyright is claimed.

Insurance

The financial commitment in setting up a workshop makes insurance essential even if it is not always a legal requirement. The building and contents should be covered against loss through fire and other perils.

Public liability insurance provides cover for customers or other members of the public visiting the workshop who may suffer injury or damage through your alleged negligence. Your pots can also be insured against causing damage or injury. Liability insurance is in many ways the most important insurance to have. The cost of a third party claim is entirely out of your control and could be very expensive.

Consequential loss insurance covers losses which would arise if there were a fire or other catastrophe which affected the workshop and prevented normal work.

There are other insurance policies which are designed to cover a multitude of potential losses and should be considered in relation to your own situation. Beware that household insurance may not cover any trade or professional activity on the premises. Workshops which are set up in a private dwelling will need separate cover.

Business practice – book keeping

Some basic financial records should be kept on a daily basis although this may not be required by law unless the business is in a more complex form such as a limited company. This information will be needed for tax calculations and to give an overall financial picture of the business. It is important that you find a book-keeping system that suits you, which you 'enjoy' and which you will keep up to date on at least a monthly basis.

The cheapest way to set up a system is with notebooks and duplicate pads available from stationers. For those with a personal computer, simple business packages are available which will record all the necessary information needed for various financial calculations and the printing of invoices.

- *Sales invoices* These record details of goods sold and may be from a simple duplicate or triplicate pad with the top copy for the customer, one copy for your records, and a delivery note if necessary. The invoice should have serial numbers and include the date of the transaction, description of goods sold, price, and tax details if applicable. It is also useful to record the purchaser's name and contact address if the sale is for a large amount, or if it is a regular customer. This will form a useful reference which can be built into a database if you want to send out marketing information at a later date.
- *Purchase invoices* These are the invoices issued by your suppliers and they form a record of all goods and services that you have purchased. You can write cheque numbers and dates on the invoice when it is paid, to keep a record.
- *Bank cheque book counterfoils* Recording details of all cheques paid out.
- *Bank paying-in book* This forms a record of all cheques and cash paid into the bank.
- *Petty cash book* A record of all cash purchases for items which are too small for a cheque to be written, and cash drawn from the bank to meet these expenses. Receipts and invoices should also be kept relating to cash purchases.
- *Bank statements* These record all receipts and expenses and can be used to cross reference against your other records.
- *Sales tax* Most countries have some form of sales tax which is charged every time money changes hands in return for goods or services. In the United Kingdom it is VAT which has to be levied once the turnover reaches a certain level. As this threshold is quite high, very few small pottery businesses are registered for VAT. The tax is collected by the seller and passed to the government agency at regular intervals. Any tax paid by the seller for goods or materials may be reclaimed. This represents a great increase of paperwork for small businesses, with little benefit if the raw materials are only a small part of total expenses.
- *Sales day book* This brings together the information from sales invoices over a period of time and can provide a running total of sales from the workshop.
- *Purchase sales book* This records the details of purchase invoices and credit notes received and provides a total of purchases of materials and services for the workshop.

From these records it is possible to extract all of the information needed to complete a tax return. An accountant can sort out all of the records, or you can do a self-assessment. In the United Kingdom, if you are on low turnover it may be possible to submit three-line accounts showing total income, total expenditure and total pre-tax profit.

It is also possible for you or an accountant to prepare a profit and loss account and a balance sheet.

- *Profit and loss account* This shows the total sales for the year and the total expenditure for the year, broken down into useful categories, with the net annual profit.
- *Balance sheet* This is a statement of assets, including everything owned by the business, equipment, materials, profits, etc. and liabilities, including outstanding loans, overdrafts, tax provision, etc. This shows the state of the business at a given point in time.

Financial information is a valuable tool which can show strengths and weaknesses and help you to plan a successful business. Analysis of your outgoings or expenditure can make you aware of how to make your business more efficient and profitable. Working longer hours to increase production and turnover does not necessarily lead to increased profits if your business expenditure is very high.

Selling

There are several existing types of outlet for studio work including:

- Direct from the workshop or specialist ceramic fairs, where the maker is involved with meeting the customer and selling.
- Galleries and shops. Contact is made with the gallery buyer who will purchase your work. Sometimes they will offer to take work on sale or return, which means that you get paid only when the work is sold. This can be one way of building a relationship with a good outlet but is not generally good for the maker who is providing the shop or gallery with

free stock. In the case of an exhibition, however, the gallery acts as an agent for the maker, prominently displaying works to its clients.
- Trade shows provide an opportunity to show your work to people who may want to buy from you at wholesale prices so that they can sell your work through their shop, gallery or other retail outlet. The cost of a stand at one of these events can be very high but some people take enough orders to make it worthwhile and even see them through the year. It is important that you can give realistic delivery dates for this type of order and spread your workload over a period of time.
- Commissions for sculptural work come from many sources including large companies, museums, arts organisations and government departments. They may advertise in arts/crafts magazines for applications, giving details of their requirements. Commissions from individuals or smaller organisations may come directly to the maker, particularly if he or she is well known or has other similar work on show to the public.
- Working in collaboration with architects. If the commission is for a particularly large, adventurous or expensive piece such as an architectural panel, it will be important to show that you are capable of completing the work to a deadline and to the required standard. Safe methods of fixing will need to be agreed with the architect. Once the first commission has been completed satisfactorily it can be used to demonstrate your competence to others. Maquettes or drawings are

usually presented to convey the maker's ideas in detail.

- Residencies, demonstrations and lectures. These activities may well generate an income in themselves, besides providing an opportunity to display and sell work to your audience. It is a good chance to promote yourself and your work by talking about your ideas, techniques and materials.

Some people who work with clay have a flexible attitude to what they produce and freely adapt to market demands. Others prefer to work on specific ideas and forms which are important to them personally but may or may not sell well. They are often prepared to find other sources of income in addition to selling their work. Related work could include part-time teaching, lecturing, or residential courses at their workshops.

Publicity and marketing material

New customers and selling opportunities can be generated through good publicity and marketing material. With all three-dimensional forms it is necessary to use two-dimensional images to show the work to a large number of people.

Photography
There will be many occasions when you will need to have good quality photographs.

Images of your work will be required for:-
- Magazines, books and catalogues.
- Postcards, leaflets and other publicity material.
- Applications for awards, prizes, grants and other competitions.
- Applications for selected craft fairs.

- Applications and interviews for courses.
- Showing work to potential customers.
- Presenting your work on the Internet.

Slides have been considered better than prints as they provide the finest detail and are still required for some situations such as publishing. Digital images are however becoming increasingly acceptable as the technology improves. It is now possible to have slides made from a digital image.

Before you proceed have a critical look at magazines and books featuring photographs of pots to see how photographers have managed to capture aspects of glaze and form.

If you wish to use a professional photographer, ask other makers to recommend someone and see examples of their previous work. Not all photographers have experience of working with ceramics and they can cost a lot of money to hire. If this is outside your budget you may consider taking some photographs yourself.

- Whether you decide to use a traditional film camera or digital you will need a camera which allows you to look through the lens and focus on objects close to you.
- A good system for film is the 35mm. single lens reflex camera (SLR).
- A digital camera should have at least a 3x optical zoom lens and more than 4 megapixel ccd. Some publications will require a high definition image.
- Take the pictures outside in natural light, overcast skies are best, or use a photographic light cube made of fabric that diffuses light and reduces reflections.
- Mount the camera on a tripod.
- Graded backgrounds give good effects

and are available from photographic shops.

- Select the smallest possible aperture and a long exposure time.
- With traditional film use one with a rating of 60 or 100 asa.

Digital cameras are rapidly overtaking those using film. They work in the same way as a conventional camera except that the image is saved electronically and can be down loaded onto a computer where they can easily be edited and incorporated into documents, publicity and presentation material. The same images can also be sent by email and used on the internet. Desktop printers can produce material of an excellent quality and can be used for experimentation and trials as well as larger print runs.

Web Sites

With access to the internet increasing rapidly web sites have become a valuable publicity tool for the potter. There are exciting possibilities for showing work to a wider audience. In most cases this facility is not used as a form of direct selling as individual work is usually best seen 'in the round'. It has however become an important point of reference that can provide images of current work, new ideas and information about where the work can be seen and bought. Background information about the maker can be included along with details of the workshop,making processes involved, and where the workshop is situated.

- The individual www.web address may include your company name and a suffix such as .com, .co.uk etc. The small annual fee involved in registering the address ensures that no other company can use it. This information can be included in your letterhead and other publicity material.
- Basic software packages for building websites use templates which allow even the novice computer operator to produce a presence on the internet in a few hours.
- There are many commercial companies that will make a site to your requirements for a fee.
- Some potters organisations will provide space on their site for members.
- It is important that the website is regularly updated with new pictures, information about exhibitions and other selling events to encourage people to revisit.
- Links can be made to sites featuring other potters, associations and likewise links made to your website from other sites specialising in ceramics or pottery. By setting up a website showing your work, anyone in the world can gain access to those images via their computer.

Presentation of publicity material is becoming increasingly important for all crafts people. Prints, slides, colour photocopies, postcards etc. will form a significant portion of expenses. In many areas there are potters' groups and/or craft organisations that hold joint shows or produce joint publicity material. These can be useful in providing services that you cannot afford on your own, as well as being a good way to meet fellow craftspeople.

Chapter Six
Potter's Workshops

Feé Halsted-Berning and the Ardmore Studios

Mooi River, Kwazulu Natal, South Africa

Ardmore Studios were established by Feé Halsted-Berning who is a successful South African ceramic artist with work in major collections throughout the country, including the South African National Gallery in Capetown, the Johannesburg Art Gallery, the UNISA Art Gallery in Pretoria and the Durban Gallery as well as in private collections throughout Africa, Europe and the USA. In 1985 she founded the Ardmore

Above Ardmore studio against the backdrop of the Drakensberg mountains. Photo: Feé Halstead-Berning
Left Bonnie Ntshalintshali outside Ardmore.

Ceramic Art Studio, a self-help studio for local artists. Today, 40 Zulu and Sotho artists are represented, producing a mixture of ceramic sculpture, wall reliefs and unique functional ware. Feé trains a group of local women to hand build and throw forms as well as to decorate.

This workshop was converted from old stables to allow room for tables and work spaces. It is constructed from stone, with large windows at one end and along the sides, beneath a tin roof. Much of the work is made from local red clays which are then painted with white

67

Above Hoopoe bowl by Bonnie
Ntshalintshali, 18 x 8 in. (46 x 20 cm)

Opposite, above Moses and Nathaniel
unpacking the kiln.
Opposite, below Ardmore Studio painters
working on the floor.
Photos: Feé Halstead-Berning

slip before being decorated when
leatherhard. White earthenware is used
for the Ardmore-thrown domestic ware.
Scraps are recycled in a bucket with
water and then poured out on to plaster
bats, wedged and stored in an old fridge.

Firing is carried out in two electric
kilns which produce the consistently
even temperatures particularly required
for glazed work.

Apart from the kilns and a slab roller,
there is very little equipment in the
workshop. Small tools are made from
anything found lying around, such as
sticks, toothpicks and pieces of metal.

There is a display area at the studio
which sells about 50% of the work, and
the remainder goes to galleries in Africa,
with some being shown as far afield as
Europe and Japan.

Arabella Ark (formerly known as Gail Bakutis)

O'ahu Waianae, Hawaii

Arabella Ark creates both functional and decorative pieces, using porcelain for three-dimensional work, and paper clay for wall pieces. She uses the whole range of firing temperatures, using electric kilns for oxidation, gas kilns for reduction, and specialises in the raku firing of large-scale, architectural vessels. She also makes Japanese style tableware, lidded boxes, vases, ornamental and functional teapots, sculptural vessels and wall hangings.

The staggering beauty of the Hawaiian islands has been a constant source of inspiration for Arabella. Colours and textures are taken from the sea, sunsets, landscape, and the volcanic rock formations.

The workshop is situated at her home and has four components: finished pieces are displayed for clients to view and purchase from a gallery in the house; a storage area for supplies, equipment and chemicals; a raku firing area which opens on to the beach and sea, ideal for those cooling dips; and a studio space for creating greenware, teaching workshops, firing gas and electric kilns, mixing and glazing ware,

and cleaning up. Because of the warm climate, the studio has open sides which allow cooling breezes to flow through. Waterproof screens can be pulled across in wet weather.

All work is hand built using slabs. Arabella has developed her own clay bodies to suit her own way of working. Her requirements include: the ability to fire the same body to both raku and cone 10 temperatures; whiteness; strength for joining; resistance to cracking and warping in drying and firing; resistance to thermal shock; and translucence at cone 10 for functional ware. These demands are satisfied by a special clay body based on porcelain, which gives the whiteness and high temperature qualities. This is made up for her to her recipe, by a clay supplier.

For wall pieces, the porcelain body is combined in powdered form with large quantities of various grogs and kyanite. Recycled paper in pulp form is added to this mixture in the ratio of ⅔ clay to ⅓ paper pulp along with small amounts of sodium silicate and vinegar.

Careful use of every bit of prepared clay minimises the amount of reclaimed clay. Leftovers are wedged, put in a

Above Removing raku kiln ring before reduction.
Above, right Rolling reduction chamber with open door around kiln.
Right Raku equipment used by Arabella Ark, including fire suit and hood, variety of gloves, tongs, respirator, kilns, burners, propane bottles and reduction chamber.
Photos: Arabella Ark

plastic bag with some water and used again in a few days.

A top-loading electric kiln, (8 cu. ft. (226 *l.*)) and updraught hardbrick gas kiln (24 cu. ft. (614 *l.*)) are used for bisque firings. Arabella designed her own raku kilns which are custom-made with thermal fibre and galvanised metal in the form of rectangular rings without bases. The base is a copper dish filled with fibre and the rings are stacked up on top of this, the number of rings being adjusted to suit the size of work to be fired.

When firing pieces of work which are too heavy to lift from the kiln with tongs

'Sunset Tea Temple' by Arabella Ark. Photo: Arabella Ark

in the normal way, Arabella Ark wears a heatproof airport firefighter's suit, complete with headgear, visor and wire mitts. The red-hot work is then lifted from the kiln by hand and placed in a reducing chamber. For pieces that are heavier than 80 lb. (36 kg.) she has designed a special rolling reduction chamber which is pushed into position over the kiln hearth after the kiln rings have been removed. Cardboard, dried palm fronds and banana leaves are used in preference to sawdust to produce a reducing atmosphere.

Overnight pit firings are carried out on the beach in front of her house, using an old restaurant stove hood which is later covered with metal roofing sheets to slow down cooling.

Slab rollers are an important feature in the workshop and are in regular use. Two models, one 15 in. (38 cm) wide and one 20 in. (51 cm) wide are heavily relied on to produce material for production work. A compressor and heavy duty stainless steel spray gun are used to spray glazes on the larger pieces. Paper clay is mixed in plastic buckets using a big power drill with a double-bladed paint mixer. A smaller 15 mm drill with a cup mixer is used to prepare glazes.

Arabella Ark sells her work through various outlets. Her smaller pieces are sold through museum gift shops. Small and larger pieces are sold in retail and hotel galleries in the islands and on mainland USA. Large pieces and murals are also commissioned for placement in banks and other public places. About half of her work is sold through an annual studio sale. Recently Arabella has established an internet website to promote her work which displays pictures and contact information for customers. Arabella has now established a new workshop near Hana, on the island of Maui, Hawaii.

Kate Malone and the Balls Pond Road Studios

London, England

This new, custom-built studio is set in a cobbled mews behind one of the oldest terraces in London's East End. The well-lit, two-storey building has specially commissioned metal doors which symbolise earth, wind, fire and water. Conceived and built by Kate Malone and Graham Inglefield, Balls Pond Road Studio provides work spaces for 10–14 potters whose work range from sculptural to decorative, and architectural to domestic.

Kate Malone, who makes huge pots, requires a large kiln to fire them in and developed the studio around the needs of the kiln, in some spare land behind her house. She bought the kiln with a 50% grant from the Crafts Council and now manages the whole of the Balls Pond Studio Road building.

With so many people using the

Each member has their own workspace and storage space.

studio, it is important that there are ground rules and that all members abide by them. A prerequisite for all potential members is that they should sign a legally binding agreement, setting out exactly what will be provided for, and what is expected of members. This includes the way members treat the studio and behave toward others. The cost of running the studio is shared between all the members by way of a monthly fee.

Kilns, including the very large electric trolley kiln, are rented out to members. A charge is made for each firing plus the cost of electricity. This covers all maintenance costs and ensures that the kilns are fully functional at all times.

The studio also has a display area where members' work is represented. Exhibitions are organised by the group, who share the necessary organisational work and costs of publicity material. An extensive mailing list has been built up of past and potential customers who may be invited to private viewings. During exhibition time the top floor workspaces are cleared completely, giving a large display area.

Many of the studio members have recently graduated from college courses and this system of a shared workshop

represents good value. Setting up a studio can often involve a considerable financial outlay, particularly if a large kiln and an inner city workspace are needed. Shared workshops enable ex-students and others to continue to develop their work, whilst enjoying good facilities and contact with other makers. Other benefits include the opportunity to buy materials in bulk and save on delivery costs, the sharing of expertise and information, and the costs of outside services such as photographic sessions.

Some spaces are rented by two members who divide the time between them. This would suit someone with a part-time job or other commitments such as a young family, and with limited time to make pots.

Kate Malone has a workspace in the studio. She is best known for her bold sculptural ceramics in the form of fish, lobsters, underwater plants, pumpkins and pineapples. Her output is very wide-ranging. She works concurrently on

Above The kiln room. Charges for kiln firings are used to cover maintenance costs.
Opposite Specially commissioned steel doors depicting earth, wind, fire and water.
Below A display area shows examples of members' work.

one-off studio pots, limited edition ceramics and serial produced wares, as well as designing for industrial production for a factory in Stoke-on-Trent. Many of the pieces she produces are on a larger-than-life scale, and their visual impact is one of bold experimentation using multi-coloured and multi-layered glazes. Recently Kate has been working with crystalline glazes.

Andy Blick

Vancouver, Canada

Andy Blick runs a workshop in the centre of the city of Vancouver, producing tiles and mouldings for residential and commercial situations, both interior and exterior. These are all designed, developed and produced to

Hand-formed tiles designed for a specific site. Photo: Andy Blick

order for interior designers and architects, often for specific sites. Andy first trained on the Harrow pottery course in London, which produced many stimulating potters in the 1960s and 1970s. He still applies many of his initial approaches and ideas to his work although he has moved away from making pots. Andy manages all of the processes used, and although he employs others to help with production, much of the work carried out in the workshop relies on his hand in some way.

A variety of production techniques are used, including hand-pressmoulding, extruding, hydraulic pressing, throwing, jiggering, hand modelling, and custom cutting using jigs and profile cutters. These procedures are often combined to produce specific effects, and all of the necessary models, moulds, profiles and cutting jigs are developed and made in the studio.

Clay bodies are custom-mixed to

specific formulations and consistencies by a clay supplier. The body used for pressing includes talc to lower the firing temperature, and a fine white grog to assist even drying and reduce shrinkage. This is prepared to a consistency which is stiffer than that used for throwing. The extruding body is of a similar formulation but is slightly stiffer with no grog. Terracotta and porcelain are occasionally used. These clays are fired to a mid-temperature range to access a broad spectrum of colour.

The workshop can be set up to accommodate changes in production. The flexibility is provided by movable benches, extrusion systems etc. which can be set up in various configurations. Jigs of different sizes, for cutting and measuring extruded lengths of clay, are used on top of workbenches. Some processes require two people working together, others work independently. Compressed air is provided to all points to assist in the removal of clay forms from pressmoulds. Fixed extraction is provided for spray booth, kilns and dry mixing areas. All kilns are electric with programmable controllers and

Left Cutting extrusions to length using a simple jig.
Below Simple jigs are used to assist production.

Top Pressed tiles drying on racks.
Above Open stacking of pressed tiles reduces warping during firing.

'kiln-sitters'. These are controllers which detect the melting of a pyrometric bar inside the kiln, thereby determining the cut-off temperature. Andy has developed methods for firing large relief mouldings without distortion by using the minimum amount of kiln furniture, allowing for better heat circulation and reduced cooling time. The faster firing cycle also saves fuel and money.

Industrial tile production is usually geared up for very large production runs which are difficult to change due to the high costs of re-tooling. The flexibility of Andy Blick's workshop is a great asset. He is able to tailor his production to suit the requirements of designers and architects, providing special shapes such as corner tiles in a range of glazes. Simple moulds and jigs can be prepared and new production runs set up at short notice. Work is also sold from specialised showrooms in the USA and from the workshop showroom but is strictly wholesale.

Esias Bosch

White River, Northern Province, South Africa

Esias Bosch worked and trained with the influential Michael Cardew at Winchcombe Pottery in England. He is now involved with his son Anton and daughter Esra in the pottery business which he established during the 1960s. This is his second workshop, which came about following a decision to move out of the city where he occupied a small rented studio.

Esias started the pottery with two rooms, a kick wheel and one large wood kiln, and has continued to expand until today the workshop covers about 8000 sq. ft. (750 m²). Situated in a semi-tropical area with a good climate, lush vegetation and beautiful scenery, it also has a good wood supply and is not far from feldspar and silica mines. Smooth concrete and brick floors ensure easy cleaning, keeping dust to a minimum. They also allow the easy movement of wheeled racks and tables carrying pots from the glaze area to the kilns.

Esias produces immense painted porcelain panels, decorated with images of wild life, which are up to 8 x 4 ft. (2.5 m x 1.25 m) and only ½ in. (13 mm) thick. Esra produces decorated domestic ware and large dishes and Anton makes mostly thrown and decorated individual pieces.

Clay bodies used include a simple middle range body for Esra's domestic ware, stoneware for Anton, a translucent porcelain and a special porcelain for the large panels. For this climate the body has to be fairly open to accommodate quick drying. Scraps are

Working on a typical large panel 8 x 4 ft. (2.5 x 1.25 m). Photo: Esias Bosch

Top Vases by Anton Bosch.
Above Decorated dish by Esra Bosch 3 ft. (1 m wide). Photos: Esias Bosch

recycled by mixing in a blunger before drying and then putting through a pugmill.

Esias' panels are made by laminating and firing layers of material to make a single, flexible tile resistant to cracking and breaking. They are fired to 1400°C (2552°F) with an amazingly low shrinkage rate of 1.5%. Each panel is supported on a specially constructed easel and the decoration is created by applying colour and glaze in layers. The panel is refired between each layer of decoration, up to eight or nine times over a period of three or four months, until the desired effect is achieved. Esra paints domestic ware with brush and sponge and produces huge bowls and dishes of up to 3 ft. (1 m) long by pressing over biscuit moulds.

Esias has built his own wheels, a pugmill, kilns and a large slab roller. He prefers to make his own equipment but is aware that his own time is expensive and that consequently it is sometimes better to buy. The workshop also uses a blunger, a ball mill and a clay mixer. The slab roller, which is used by Esias to prepare clay for his large panels, is run by an electric motor geared down to provide a steady speed with plenty of torque.

An extensive range of kilns, mostly built by Esias himself, serve the pottery. The 200 cu. ft. (5500 *l.*) oil-fired trolley kiln is used for domestic ware production, the work being packed easily with the trolley pulled out. Glaze colour

varies in this and another, smaller, oil kiln but is more consistent in two smaller trolley kilns powered by electricity.

The great ingenuity and technical ability of Esias Bosch is shown in the two electric top-loading kilns, designed and built to fire large porcelain panels. These are shallow, steel-framed structures with flat lids which are raised with help from a system of counter weights, wires and pulleys.

Most of Esias' work is now

Top Motorised slab roller used to prepare large porcelain panels.
Above Esias Bosch with the electric kilns which he designed to fire his large porcelain panels. Photos: Esias Bosch

commissioned, often from architects, and he sells very little through shops and galleries. About 90% of the remaining pottery output is sold from the two display areas at the studio, and the rest through mixed exhibitions and commissions.

Richard Dewar

Brittany, France

Richard Dewar has set up a workshop in the southern part of Brittany, France, where he works alone, producing salt-glazed stoneware. His pots are based on functional forms and range from short runs of a particular piece to individual one-off decorative objects. Everything is made on the wheel initially, although much time is spent in finishing when forms are altered; handles and spouts and other decorative features added; and slips and glazes applied.

The workshop is situated in an old cow shed which is attached to one side of an enormous barn. It is a long thin room with storage shelves down one side and working space on the other. The kiln is situated in an adjoining outbuilding. A matching space on the opposite side of the barn houses a gallery/display area for retail sales. Richard Dewar lives on the same premises and he feels this is vital for long firings and out-of-hours customers. The rural location provides space and tranquillity, whilst the stone buildings are warm in winter and cool in

Top Workshop and kiln room on the left, living accommodation with hunting tower on the right.
Above Richard Dewar's thrown and altered lidded form. Salt-glazed with slip and glaze decoration. Photos: Richard Dewar

summer. The workshop is spacious and light and airy with windows looking out onto the garden and fish pond.

One of the striking things about Richard Dewar's workshop is the lack of equipment and gadgets found in many

82

workshops. In fact he works with very few tools, preferring to keep everything as simple as possible. His main wheel is a Leach-type kick wheel which he made as a student. This is enjoyed for its near silent operation which allows the operator to listen to the radio while throwing.

The stoneware clay (F100) comes from the Saint-Amand-en-Puisaye region of France, and is high in silica and low in iron, making it good for salt-glazing. Scrap clay is wetted down in plastic bins and recycled using plaster bats. When carried out on a weekly basis the system works well. Slips and glazes are prepared in the workshop using a simple balance.

The 70 cu. ft. (2000 l.) oil-fired, downdraught kiln was built by Richard Dewar. The basic structure consists of a brick cube with a steel frame and tie-bars which support the arch. Two burners are situated at the front of the kiln, firing towards the back. He fires the kiln six times each year. All pots are once-fired to a temperature of about 1300°C (2372°F). This takes about 17 hours before reduction is begun. Reduction itself lasts a further 5 hours. Salt is introduced into the kiln over the last 1½ hours using a piece of angle iron as a 'spoon' to pour it into the firebox. This produces the typical salt glaze, orange-peel effect on any exposed clay surface and encourages the slips and glazes to run down vertical surfaces.

When he set up his first workshop Richard was prepared to take on a

Left, above One wall of the workshop is given over to shelves for drying work ready for firing.
Left Salt is introduced into the kiln on a piece of angle iron during the last 1½ hours of the firing. Photos: Richard Dewar

variety of work in order to make a living, including repetition throwing of honey pots for a honey producer. Now that he is established, he is able to make the type of pots which interest him, and find outlets for them. About 50% of his work is sold directly to the public from the workshop display. Potters' markets take a further 25% and galleries, exhibitions and shops take the remaining 25%. Advertising is kept to a minimum, although road signs have been erected at many points in the area and publicity material distributed locally.

Below Unfired pots packed in the kiln shortly before the door, or wicket, is bricked up. Each piece is standing on small wads of alumina and china clay to prevent it sticking to the shelf.
Left After the firing the pots are transformed. These kiln shelves are made of silicon carbide. Photos: Richard Dewar

Geoff Fuller

The Three Stags' Heads, Derbyshire, England

Geoff Fuller has found a building which allows him to combine the business of making pots with the running of a small specialist public house called the Three Stags' Heads in the wilds of the Derbyshire Peak District. At first sight the two roles may seem to be very different but Geoff Fuller finds these activities quite compatible. The Three Stags' Heads provides distinct beers and food for a particular group of specialist consumers and his pottery is bought by another group of customers who enjoy his individual way of making pottery.

The building was originally used as a pub and farmhouse, with some of the main structure of the house built as accommodation for livestock. It remains quite unspoiled and unaltered by modernisation, lending itself well to its new dual functions.

Geoff produces two main types of work, both made from red earthenware clay and influenced by early English country pottery. The standard ware is a range of simple functional dishes decorated with a variety of images drawn with trailed, coloured slip. These are designed by Geoff and made by him and other employees for use and sale through the pub and other outlets. He also makes more individual work, often functional mugs, jugs and dishes, or modelled seated figures and dogs, decorated with slips and a clear earthenware glaze.

The workshop at the Three Stags' Heads is a long room, previously the milking parlour of the farm, and still retaining some original features such as the low walls used to divide the cattle and the concrete floors and walls

designed to assist cleaning after milking. Geoff uses very little equipment and the overall tone of the workshop is of order and purpose. The only objects to be found are those required for making pottery.

Red clay is bought ready-prepared from a potters' suppliers and used from the bag without additions. Geoff's wheel is a small Shimpo type, set in a Japanese style throwing table cum seat, which allows easy access to tools and plenty of space for pot boards. The wheel head has been drilled to take the three wooden studs which are fixed to the throwing bats. Working light comes from a window above the throwing area, plus a desk light. There are few throwing tools and they have all been made by Geoff, each one a familiar old friend with particular uses when throwing.

Further along the workshop at the next window is the decorating area with a collection of brushes and slip trailers, again some specially made to produce particular lines or effects with the decorating slips.

Pots which are awaiting decoration or

Above The Three Stags' Heads Inn and pottery, Derbyshire, England.
Right Small covered bowl. Photos: Geoff Fuller

are drying are kept on pot boards which are rested on the wooden pegs located along the length of the workshop. Drying can be a problem during the winter months, as the large workshop space has been difficult to heat with the existing solid fuel stove. Production thus often slows down as shelves fill up with damp pots. Geoff hopes that this situation will be improved with the provision of central heating radiators. The kiln, situated in an adjoining room is an electric 8 cu. ft.(227 l.) front loader which uses economy rate electricity.

The standard ware is used in the pub to serve food, and generates a great deal of interest among customers there. There is a small display and they can even buy the plate they have just eaten from! The remainder of the standard ware is bought for resale in craft shops. At present Geoff sells most of his individual work through galleries but

87

would like to increase the amount he sells directly from the pottery as he is increasingly concerned with the mark-up charged, particularly by London galleries. He hopes to convert the large space above the workshop into a gallery to accommodate the increasing number of customers who visit the workshop.

Top The workshop utilises the existing cow stalls which divide the space into throwing, clay preparation and glazing bays.
Above The throwing bench is a seat and table for holding clay, water, tools and pots. Bats are stacked ready for the next throwing session.

Peter Hayes

Bath, England

The elegant Georgian city of Bath has a wealth of interesting buildings and here Peter Hayes has discovered a most unusual setting for his workshop. One of the main bridges over the river Avon has four toll houses, one at each corner. These may have been used at one time to collect tolls from travellers crossing the bridge but now one of them has become a workshop and gallery.

Peter makes sculptural ceramic forms reminiscent of standing stones or enlarged versions of pebbles polished by the sea.

The building consists of three square rooms above one another. The top room, at bridge level, is the gallery with a display of Peter's work. A spiral stair leads down to the middle floor which is the main workshop. Moulds and materials are stored here along with a slab roller. Peter works at a window which opens on to the river below. The ground floor is used as the kiln room with two oval electric top-loading kilns. A door leads to the outside – a small terrace at river level with some wooden decking built over the water. This space is used for raku firing.

Peter designs and makes plaster moulds to produce the basic forms for his sculptures. Clay is prepared for this on a slab roller, pressed into the two halves of the moulds which are then aligned and pushed together. Some shapes allow room for a hand to reach inside to smooth and strengthen the join while others need to be worked with a long stick. The outside is burnished and worked to produce both smooth and textured areas.

After biscuit firing, oxides are rubbed into the surface and the piece is refired

Peter Hayes' converted toll house on the banks of the river Avon in Bath.

Above Peter Hayes working on a press-moulded form by an open window.
Left Kiln yard with fibre-lined raku kilns.
Right Three single rooms above each other constitute gallery, workroom and kiln room. The kiln yard provides access to the river, itself used as a part of the making process.

in a raku kiln and subjected to a reduction atmosphere which darkens the surface. Peter is interested in achieving surfaces that look as if they are weathered and worn by age. He has developed a method of speeding up this process by taking sculptures up the river in a rowing boat which is kept moored at the workshop. At various places in the river he sinks the sculptures onto the river bed and leaves them there to weather. At a later date, when he fishes them up, they have adopted a warm coloured tint.

The kiln yard, just above river level, has several propane-fired raku kilns. They are all insulated with ceramic fibre and of the 'top hat' type. The largest kiln is made from an oil drum. The weight and size of this kiln makes it unsuitable for lifting by hand and a simple gantry and pulley system has been built next to it.

Peter sells most of his work through exhibitions and galleries in Great Britain and abroad. He also attends potter's fairs such as the 'Earth and Fire' fair at Rufford, Nottinghamshire. This fair, which is organised by the Craft Potters' Association of Great Britain, includes an opportunity for potters to demonstrate their making processes and here Peter has been able to demonstrate his raku technique to potential customers.

Natural lighting and a light background emphasise these forms in the gallery.

Simon Hulbert and Brook Street Pottery

Hay-on-Wye, Wales

Established by Simon Hulbert and Sara Bowie in the Welsh market town of Hay-on-Wye, Brook Street Pottery is both pottery workshop and gallery. Simon produces individual terracotta garden pots, and Sara runs the gallery which sells a range of contemporary ceramics and other crafts.

Simon sometimes develops ideas for his work by using an Apple Macintosh computer with 3-D design software. This allows him to view the intended form from all sides, quickly alter shapes, and new and unexpected interpretations of the original idea often arise. A lifesize working drawing is produced before any work is started and when the piece is to be a commission, may be used as a basis for discussion with a client. The drawing

may be produced directly from the computer or freehand. Templates are made from this drawing 11.5% oversize to allow for shrinkage.

Plaster pressmoulding, coiling and throwing are all used and sometimes techniques are combined in one vessel. The different parts of the form are allowed to dry to a leatherhard state before joining. Handles are usually pulled and other details modelled. Surfaces are often covered with terra sigillata which gives a soft sheen. The creases and folds which occur in pressmoulded forms are accentuated by rubbing glaze into them.

A few basic hand tools are needed: plastic profiles and ribs during throwing; metal kidneys; broken hacksaw blades;

Coiled forms are worked in rotation, with each piece taken as far as possible before it needs to firm up, ready for the next stage.

and wooden modelling tools to refine and join the forms.

If the vessel is to be coiled, the pugmill (fitted with a die) is used to produce enough coils for the day. These are then put on to boards and covered with polythene to keep them damp.

The clay body is a blend of grogged red earthenware with crank body – a very coarse refractory clay. The two clays, Valentine's red clay and crank clay in a 2:1 ratio, are mixed in a pugmill. The red earthenware gives a terracotta colour whilst the crank allows

94

the body to be fired to a higher temperature. The grog content of the body allows the pots to dry out evenly, reducing the risk of cracking and warping. This is particularly important for larger pieces which can be 3 ft. (1 m) or more high.

The workshop consists of one large room in which all processes are carried out. Just inside a pair of double doors, which give access to the road outside, is the clay storage and preparation area. A vertical pugmill is bolted to the wall. A washing machine has been installed so that dirty overalls and throwing towels can be cleaned in the workshop. A large bench is situated in the middle of the room for pressmoulding and assembling pots. Next to this are two electric wheels. The gas-fired trolley kiln is against the

Left Inlaid terracotta urn, 24 in. (60 cm).
Below Workshop interior showing clay and glaze material storage. The washing machine is used for washing throwing towels and overalls.

back wall, with its flue going up through the ceiling.

Simon has designed and built the kiln specifically for the type of work he is now producing. A picture is shown in the section on kilns. Larger garden pots can be easily loaded on to the trolley even if two people are needed to lift them. Either side of the kiln chamber are two atmospheric, natural gas burners fitted with control valves and pressure gauges. The firings are taken slowly, because of the large scale of much of the work, and take two days to reach a top temperature of 1180–1200°C (2156-2192°F). At this temperature the clay is vitrified. To vary the fired clay surface with flashing effects, Simon places salt 'bombs' in the kiln. These are small containers, often kiln props, which have been filled with salt and placed among the pots. The salt vaporises and forms a glaze by combining with silica in the clay.

The gallery at Brook Street Pottery sells about 80% of the output from the

Ground floor of gallery showing a display of work by Simon Hulbert.

workshop, the remainder going to exhibitions and selected potters' markets. The sale of other potters' work, from the gallery stock and through special exhibitions, provides additional income to the business. Simon also undertakes some teaching sessions on college ceramics courses.

Walter Keeler

Penault, Wales

Walter Keeler had been making pots for over 20 years at his present pottery, an old farmhouse complete with outbuildings, set in the unspoiled country near Monmouth. Although Walter has a background of producing repetition domestic ware he now makes more individual pieces. His characteristic clear, crisp, wheel-thrown forms are later altered and assembled into functional jugs, mugs, teapots and storage jars which are fired in either salt glaze or earthenware kilns.

The farm outbuildings have been used for throwing, glazing and display of finished work without any major structural changes being carried out. A recent development, however, has been the decision by Walter to design and build a completely new workshop. Positioned on one side of the kiln yard the new space provides an ideal environment for him to throw and assemble his pots.

The new room designed by Walter has a single pitch roof covered with old pantiles and includes two roof lights. The whole of the front wall is made from floor to ceiling windows which allow the light to pour into the studio. Inside there is an almost complete absence of clutter. The white walls are virtually free of those shelving systems and storage areas found in many studios. This clarity

emphasises the work in progress and the direct lighting emphasises the pottery form.

By the kick wheel is a small trolley, used to carry the thrown sections to a single turntable on a base by the window. Here Walter cuts and assembles the pots and applies handles. A series of drying shelves (shown in the previous chapter on workshop layout) are positioned above a small wood stove in the corner. This workspace satisfies the need to focus on individual pieces and small batches of work. There are no concessions made to mass-production.

All thrown forms are made on a kick wheel, designed by Dave Cohen and made by Keltneyburn Kickwheels, Perthshire, Scotland. The simple design requires the operator to kick the flywheel directly, and is quiet and smooth in operation. Skills developed during Walter's time making repetition tableware are just as valuable in the production of more individual pieces.

Walter Keeler designed this workshop for throwing and assembling his pots.

The fluency of his making is complemented by the ability to develop processes and equipment which improve his efficiency and save time. Plastic profiles, cut from hard plastic sheet, are used to give a neat series of moulded ridges which articulate the form. Such a profile is used during throwing, and also on the assembled piece, by pulling it around the pot, improving the join between wall and base. A special cutting tool, formed from a small block of wood and a sharpened nail, is run around the base of a pot to give a perfectly level edge. Another tool consists of a row of sharpened nails which are used to score surfaces prior to joining. Hollow extrusions are often used for handles, and pressmoulds for spouts and handles. Experiments with various making processes are part of a continuous search to explore the qualities of clay.

97

For salt glazing, a biscuit slip is added to some parts of the pot and stains sprayed over the complete piece. The area coated by slip gives a different texture to the salt glaze compared with the area only covered by the stain.

Walter Keeler uses a dough mixer to blend his clay body for salt glaze. The body is made from:

HVAR Ball Clay   112 lb. (50 kg)
  (Watts Blake and Bearne)
Sand, 80s mesh   13 lb. (6 kg)
  (Arnolds)
This is mixed in a dough mixer with water prior to adding:
1124 prepared body   55.5 lb. (25 kg)
  (Potclays)

It is then mixed again until thoroughly blended.

Left Crabstock jug on stand with Sansai decoration (1060°C (1940°F)).

Above The workshop has excellent natural lighting, and the absence of unnecessary clutter focuses attention on the pots being made.

Opposite below A simple kick wheel is used for all thrown forms. The ample tray holds a good supply of hand tools.

Right An old tea trolley is very useful when moving work around the studio.

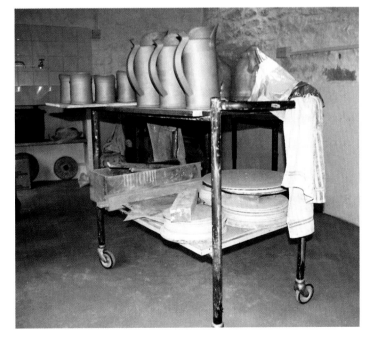

99

The kiln yard with the smaller, 8 cu. ft. (227 l.) oil fired salt kiln.

Biscuit slip (engobe):

Feldspar	60
China clay	40

Interior Glaze (Phil Wood)

Cornish stone	70
Wollastonite	30
Red Iron Oxide	8

Two kilns are used for salt glazing, a 32 cu. ft. (885 l.) and another of 8 cu. ft. (227 l.). The smaller kiln is favoured as it gives more frequent firings. They are both catenary arch structures made of heavy refractory bricks covered by 2 in. (5 cm) of ceramic fibre. Two oil burners are used on each kiln, set at opposite corners to give maximum turbulence for salt glazing and even heating. The burners on the larger kiln are commercial 'Swirlamiser' burners, the smaller kiln runs with one home-made burner. Both use compressed air to vaporise the heating oil. A small front loading electric kiln is used for the recent earthenware pieces.

Some retail sales are made from the workshop although Walter does not have a showroom or gallery as such. The majority of work is sold through craft galleries or by exhibition and is represented in several major collections in the UK and abroad. Walter also attends some of the potters' fairs. He takes his pots in a small box-trailer towed behind his car. This is small enough to be parked very close to the market stall.

Anna Lambert

Keighley, Yorkshire Dales, England

Anna Lambert produces finely made, hand-built earthenware. She uses coiling, pinching and modelling techniques to make a range of domestic forms including candlesticks, egg cups, toast racks and large plates. These are painted with underglaze colour which emphasises the form and surface texture. She says that her aim is to 'combine function with evocative and observed images of country life to produce joyful individual pieces.'

Anna's workshop is situated on the fringe of a small village which is itself on the edge of the Yorkshire Dales. The building, which is built into a hill, was once a coach house for a large manor

Anna Lambert's workshop, a converted coach house on the edge of the Yorkshire Dales.

house and is now converted into smaller units. Anna uses an area on the first floor which is level with the ground at the back owing to the slope of the hill. The room is a large, open and flexible space, without any fixed partitions or other obstructions but it has been carefully organised to accommodate the particular requirements of her work. Each area is used for a particular purpose – coiling, extruding, painting, glazing, etc.

Decoration is carried out by a window, which gives the best light for close work and is surrounded by photographs and other source material which Anna draws upon for colours and

prepared earthenware body and 'T' material (light coloured high temperature body with molochite sand) in a 2:1 ratio. This blend provides a strong, white body with good joining and drying properties, used for coiled, slabbed and extruded forms. Each piece is built in stages, often beginning with pinching, with coils added a few at a time and refined by scraping as they dry. The larger shapes such as the main components of complex candelabra are allowed to dry slightly before joining. Decoration in the form of modelled farm animals and fish are worked directly on to the surface of forms which have been damped then wrapped and allowed to stand for a while. A tall, floor-mounted whirler is used to turn work around while the underglaze decoration is applied. A disc mounted on the shaft, below the turntable top, allows it to be rotated with one hand and decoration applied with the other. Finished pieces are transferred to roofing slates and dried on a large centrally-placed rack which also serves as a holding area for fired work prior to packing and despatch.

Firings are carried out in two modern, round top-loader electric kilns governed by a single digital pyrometer which can be switched between the kilns. This enables Anna to control her firings with precision, allowing extremely slow increases in temperature when firing slightly damp work and a timed soak at the end of the glaze firing. Biscuit firing is taken to 1080°C (1976°F) and then each piece is covered with a matt black glaze subsequently sponged off, leaving traces in textures and corners which emphasise the form. Oxides, underglaze colours and stains with gum arabic as a medium are painted on to the forms and rubbed into the surface to remove brush marks. A

Lidded jar with blackbird on holly bush, 11 in. (28 cm). Photo: Anna Lambert

forms. Images of chickens jostle with stark photographs of the Yorkshire Dales, palettes and brushes are within easy reach. A typist's chair gives good back support for the long sessions spent painting, and a banding wheel allows pieces to be turned easily without the need for constant handling.

Anna uses a mixture of commercially

Top Decorating area by window; brushes; turntable; and source material pinned on the wall.
Above Glazing bench with work ready for spraying; glaze tests mounted on the wall; and glaze materials.

Storage rack for work in progress, and finished pieces awaiting packing and despatch.

transparent glaze is applied by dipping or spraying.

One corner of the workshop is designated as the office where all the paperwork is kept. Book keeping is kept to the minimum with just a sales book and records of all purchases and orders, which are then handed on to an accountant to prepare for tax purposes.

Anna's work takes a long time to produce. The care and attention to detail that is lavished on each piece has to be reflected in the price. At the same time Anna is concerned that they should not be treated as objects, and tries to keep prices to a minimum through efficient production, good organisation, planning and the practical use of time-saving aids such as templates. Her favourite items to make have been the larger, individual items such as candelabra and bowls, and she has discovered good outlets for these in America and Europe. Most of Anna Lambert's work is sold through galleries but she also holds successful 'open workshop' weeks when the public are invited in, and the central rack is moved to one end of the workshop to provide a display of work for sale. These open workshops have dramatically improved sales in the area. Anna uses very little marketing material, preferring to rely on customers seeing her work in exhibitions. A price list and information about herself is sent out to interested galleries along with slides of her work. Anna has established a new studio near Crosshills, North Yorkshire, England.

Janet Mansfield

Gulgong, NSW, Australia

Morning View is Janet Mansfield's family farm near Gulgong in New South Wales, Australia, where she built her first anagama kiln in 1988. A variety of other kilns have been built here over the last 20 years and as there is plenty of space, there is never any need to pull down old kilns. The kiln shed roof is just extended a little further each time. During this time she has worked with both salt-glaze and anagama wood-fired kilns, producing domestic ware in the form of cups, bowls, jars, vases and plates.

The workshop itself is a pioneer's house, probably built about 1870. It measures 30 x 15 ft. (9.2 x 4.6 m) and

Workshop buildings at Morning View, Gulgong, New South Wales.

contains a small store room and a clay mixing room in addition to the main studio. Alongside it Janet has built a small bungalow for people to stay or wash or cook when they are firing. Two other buildings have also been erected, one for books and pots and the other to use as an extra workshop or display area. Janet feels that the outlook from the workshop is one of its best aspects. The wheel is under a window which looks out onto the quiet rolling hills.

Janet's two major pieces of equipment are a kick wheel and a slab roller. Her hand tools have been collected over the thirty years that she has been a potter. Some of them are favourites such as the large iron turning

Janet Mansfield's wood-fired vessel.

tool which she bought in Japan and an incising tool bought in the German salt-glaze district.

Gulgong is considered to have some of the best clays in Australia. Janet can go to the clay pits near her home and dig her own clay or she can have the local clay supplier make up a mix for her provided she orders a tonne at a time. The mix contains mostly white clay, with some of the brown clay and some of the local feldspar (called rhyspar) which is more siliceous than the standard feldspars. The brown clay has about 5% of iron in it and she usually adds 10% to the white clay so that the final mix is 0.5% iron. The rhyspar can make up to 40% of the body. Different variations of the recipe are ordered from the clay supplier depending on which type of firing it is destined for. Often a local coarse sand is added, or some of the local unmilled brick clay for texture.

All clay scraps are recycled by soaking in bins and then passing through a de-airing pugmill. Some of the recycled clay is added to the new batch and passed through the pugmill to help clay plasticity.

Most of the kilns are built out of a cheap, local white building brick. Janet has built most of the kilns herself except for some special kilns that have been built during events at Gulgong. Examples of these are John Neely's train kiln and Fred Olsen's racing car kiln. A trolley kiln which is designed for wood-fired salt glazing takes 30 hours and is fired about four times a year, the anagama takes 80 hours and is fired about once a year and the racing car kiln, which takes over 40 hours, is fired about three times a year. There are always other people to help during the kiln firings as wood kilns are labour intensive. The helpers also have some of their own pots in the kilns.

Most of Janet's work is sold through

Workshop interior.

Top Morning View kiln shed showing five wood-fired kilns.
Above Local claypits, Gulgong, New South Wales, Australia.

exhibition, either solo or group. She is also the author of several books on Australian and international ceramics, and editor of two magazines, *Ceramics:* *Art and Perception* and *Ceramics Technical.* She travels widely, taking part in international juries, symposia and workshops and is vice-president of the International Academy of Ceramics. Janet is also well known for her large gatherings of local and international potters at Morning View, Gulgong, for workshops and firing events.

Jack Troy

Huntingdon, Pennsylvania, USA

Jack Troy is a teacher, potter and writer. He bought a plot of land about 1.5 miles from the small town of Huntingdon and designed and built both house and studio himself. Jack feels that having a personalised workspace is necessary for making personalised work. Furthermore, the setting and outlook of the workshop are very important to him, with the close proximity of wildlife and the effect of the changing seasons on his surroundings.

The workshop is built into the steep wooded hillside a short distance from the house. Being dug into the hill helps insulate the workshop in both summer and winter, with additional insulation in the walls, floor and ceiling. The layout consists of a storeroom for showing finished work, a 'thinking room' that doubles as a guest space, and a large central work area, about 30 x 20 ft. (9 x 6 m).

Jack makes wheel-thrown stoneware and porcelain. The forms are often altered, to emphasise the firing effects, with egotes (throwing sticks) and bisqued stamps which he makes himself. The pots are either glazed and fired in a propane reduction kiln, glazed by the natural effect of ash from an anagama kiln, or glazed with shino glazes and placed in saggars in the anagama. He fires about half of his work in the gas kiln and the remainder with wood.

General making area with kick and electric wheels. Photo: Jack Doherty

Workshop heater with drying racks for pots.
Photo: Jack Doherty

Two clay bodies are mixed in an old dough mixer. One is a standard Grolleg porcelain made from:

Grolleg	55
Potash spar	25
Flint	25

This is used for reduction firings as well as anagama.

The other is a smooth stoneware, composed of:

Stoneware clay	50
Ball clay	25
Fireclay	10
Feldspar	7.5
Silica	7.5

Scrap clay is kept moist in plastic bags or dustbins and added to dry clay in the dough mixer before pugging.

Jack has constructed two anagama kilns, one about 200 cu. ft. (5500 *l.*) and the other 300 cu. ft. (8250 *l.*) which he uses to create special effects on the surface of his work. The cycles of oxidising and reduction, along with the effect of wood ash over a long period at high temperature, produce variations of colour and texture which cannot be achieved in any other way. Other effects are achieved in a 65 cu. ft. (1800 *l.*) propane-fired kiln which is built with high quality 'soft' insulation bricks.

Jack has exhibitions and sells his work when teaching workshops, which he does regularly. About 10–20% of sales are to 'walk-in' customers. One 3-hour sale is held each year at the workshop, always on the same Saturday in October. Jack's 20th annual sale was held in 1998 and has been described as a 'feeding frenzy'. Originally the sale was held over five days with sales spread evenly over each day. By gradually reducing the length of the sale, Jack has found that he can now sell an equivalent amount of work in only 3 hours.

Top Jack Troy examines pots from his latest firing.
Above Shino-glazed unomi lie by the kiln.
Photos: Jack Doherty

Tina Vlassopulos

London, England

Using basic hand-building techniques, Tina Vlassopulos shapes red earthenware clay into organic, flowing forms, each with its own wave-like rhythm. Her sources of inspiration are taken from objects of everyday life as well as from nature, and the result is a whole series of related pieces developing a theme.

The workshop is situated in a room which is part of a first floor flat in a residential building in north London. The working area is only about 12 x 14ft. (3.5 x 4.5 m) but is sufficient for the type of processes carried out and is well-ordered with little wasted space or clutter. The white walls, shelves and cupboards give a light and airy feel to the space, which is kept clean and free from clay dust. The lightness and simplicity of the room also provide an excellent backdrop for the pots with their bright fired terracotta or earthy unfired colours. There is little to distract from the forms themselves. Photographs and other visual source materials are arranged on the wall, and a few shelves accumulate finished work ready for the next exhibition.

One side of the room has a surface which can be used to mix slips or dry out small amounts of clay, although

Left Burnished red earthenware vessels.
Photo: Mike Abrahams
Below Workbench with current series of pots. Anglepoise lamps provide a good light source.

Storage shelves for completed pots ready for exhibition.

Tina does neither of these activities with her current work. The kiln is also situated in the same room, positioned in a bay window to ensure good ventilation during firing.

Each piece is refined by scraping from the initial coiled and slab-built vessel until the walls are of a uniform thickness. This method of working depends on the clay being at the right degree of hardness at each stage. Consequently, several pieces are started and worked on in turn as they reach the necessary state of hardness. The surface of each vessel is burnished to a soft

sheen, enhancing the rich terracotta colouring.

Tina uses very little equipment in the production of her work. She has a collection of favourite objects for scraping and burnishing, including serrated metal shapes, knives and blades. Spoons, stones and other smooth objects are used to burnish the surface, often with help from a small piece of thin polythene for the final polish. A turntable is available but much of the forming and finishing is carried out with the piece held on her knee. Sandpaper may be used to flatten bases of dry pots. Tina uses a simple beam balance bought in Greece to weigh out oxides, and a larger set of domestic scales for clay materials.

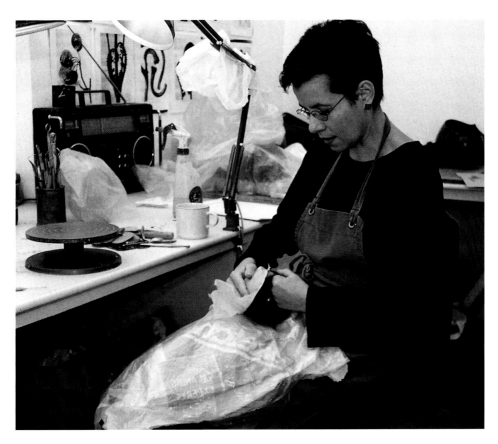

Above Tina Vlassopulos burnishing a terracotta form with thin sheets of polythene.
Right Top-loading electric kiln by the workshop window.

Grogged red earthenware clay is purchased from a pottery supplier and used straight from the bag. The grog reduces shrinkage and allows the clay to dry without cracking.

A small, top-loading electric kiln, fitted with a simple pyrometer and manual controls, is used to fire all work to 940°C (1724°F). At higher temperatures the pot would lose its burnished quality, but Tina has perfected her firings to ensure consistent results. Larger pieces are often fired on their own

Tina Vlassopulos' workshop is set up in a townhouse.

and sometimes have to be laid down at an angle to fit in the kiln. Although a larger kiln would accommodate more pieces in one firing, the process of hand building is fairly slow and the work can be fired as each piece is finished and dried. After firing each piece is heated to 100°C before polishing with clear household furniture polish.

Tina has exhibited in many solo exhibitions in London and Athens, and in group exhibitions in London, Minneapolis, Paris, Maastricht and Berlin. She does not sell from her studio, but has built a good relationship with galleries which sell her work regularly. Tina promotes her work with a professional range of publicity material including postcards and a full colour booklet about her work.

Appendix

International Craft and Potters Associations

World Crafts Council International
    c/o Pontificia Universidad Catolica de
    Chile
    El Comendador 1916, Providencia
    Santiago, Chile 6640064
    www.wccwis.gr

WCC-Europe
    World Crafts Council Europe Secretariat
    106, Rue de Nimy, B-7000 Mons
    (Belgique)
    Tel. +32 (0)65 84 64 67
    wcc-europe.org

United Kingdom

Crafts Council
    44a Pentonville Road
    London, N1 9BY
    Tel. 020 7278 7700
    www.craftscouncil.org.uk

The Craft Potters Association of Great Britain
    7 Marshall Street,
    London W1F 7EH
    Tel. 020 7437 7605
    www.cpaceramics.com

Scottish Arts Council
    12 Manor Place
    Edinburgh
    EH3 7DD
    Tel. 0131 226 6051
    www.scottisharts.org.uk

Scottish Potters Association
    www.scottishpotters.co.uk

South Wales Potters
    www.southwalespotters.org.uk

North Wales Potters
    Sue King, Ivy Cottage, Penmaenmawr
    Conwy. LL34 6HW
    www.northwalespotters.co.uk

Ireland

The Crafts Council of Ireland
    www.ccoi.ie/

The Craft Potters Society of Ireland
    ceramicsireland.org

Crafts Council of Ireland
    Castle Yard, Kilkenny, Ireland
    Tel . +353 (0)56 7761804

North America

The American Ceramic Society
    735 Ceramic Place, Suite 100
    Westerville, Ohio 43081
    Tel. 614-890-4700
    www.ceramics.org

The American Craft Council
    72 Spring Street, New York, NY 10012
    Tel. 212-274-0630
    www.craftcouncil.org

Canada

The Canadian Craft Federation
    Ontario Crafts Council, Designers Walk
    170 Bedford Road, Suite 300, Toronto,
    ON M5R 2K9
    Tel. 905 891-5928
    canadiancraftsfederation.ca

Australia

Craft Australia
Level 1 Suite 7
National Press Club
16 National Circuit
Barton ACT 2600
Tel. + 61 2 6273 0088
www.craftaus.com.au

The Potters Society of Australia
PO Box 274, Waverley, NSW 2024,
Tel. 1300 720 124
www.potteryinaustralia.com

South Africa

Ceramics Southern Africa
PO Box 2900
North Riding, 2162
Tel. +27 (0)11 791 5153
www.ceramics.org.za

Craft Council of South Africa
3 President Street, cnr. Goch Street
Newtown. P.O.Box: 57. Newtown. 2113,
Gauteng
Tel. +27 11 834 9569
www.craftcouncil.co.za

Germany

German Crafts Associaton
Windmühlstraße 3
60329 Frankfurt am Main
Germany
Tel. +49 (0)69 74 02 31
www.bundesverband-kunsthandwerk.de

Kalkspatz
Guenter Haltmayer, Dorfstr. 14,
D-17194 Klein Luckow,
Tel. +49 39933 71695
www.kalkspatz.ceramic.de

New Zealand

The New Zealand Society of Potters
http://www.nzpotters.com/
New Zealand Society of Potters (Inc.)
PO Box 31141, Christchurch

Ceramics Magazines and Periodicals

United Kingdom

Crafts
Crafts Council, 44a Pentonville Rd
London N1 9BY
Tel. 020 7278 7700
www.craftscouncil.org.uk

Ceramic Review
25 Foubert's Place, London W1F 7QF
Tel. 020 7439 3377
Fax 020 7287 9954
www.ceramic-review.co.uk

United States of America

American Ceramics
9 East 45 St, New York, NY 10017
Tel. 212 661 4397 Fax 212 661 2389

American Craft Magazine
American Crafts Council, 72 Spring St.
New York, NY 10012
Tel. 800 562 1973

Art Calendar
PO Box 199, Upper Fairmount, MD 21867
Tel. 800 597 5988 Fax 410 651 5313

Ceramics Monthly
735 Ceramic Place, Suite 100
Westerville, OH 43081
Tel. 614 794 5890
Fax 614 891 8960
www.ceramicsmonthly.org

Clay Times
15481 Second St.,PO Box 365,
Waterford, VA 20197
Tel. 540 882 3576
Fax. 540 882 4196
www.claytimes.com

Crafts Report
100 Rogers Rd, Wilmington, DE 19899
Tel. 800 777 7098
Fax 302 656 4894
www.craftsreport.com

Pottery Making Illustrated
735 Ceramic Place, Suite 100,
Westerville, OH 43081

Tel. 614 794 5890
Fax 614 891 8960
www.potterymaking.org

Professional Craft Journal
PO Box 1585, Palo Alto, CA 94302
Tel. 415 324 4156
Fax 415 327 9594

Studio Potter Network Newsletter
PO Box 70, Goffstown, NH 03045
Tel. 603 774 3582
Fax. 603 774 6313
www.studiopotter.org

Australia

Ceramics Art And Perception
120 Glenmore Rd, Paddington,
Sydney, 2021
Tel. 612 9361 5286
Fax. 612 9361 5402
www.ceramicart.com.au

Ceramics Technical
35 William St, Paddington, Sydney, 2021
www.ceramicart.com.au/technical.htm

Pottery In Australia
PO Box 274, Waverley, NSW 2024
Tel. 1300 720 124
Fax 02 9369 3742
www.potteryinaustralia.com

France

L'Atelier Société Nouvelle des Editions
Créativité
41 rue Barrault, 75013 Paris

La Ceramique Moderne
22 rue Le Brun, 75013 Paris

Germany

Keramik Magazin
Steinfelder Strasse 10,
W-8770 Lohr am Main
www.keramikmagazin.de

Neue Keramik
Steinreuschweg 2, 56203, Höhr-
Grenzhausen
Tel. 49 948 068
www.neue-keramik.de

Greece

Clay in Art International
PO Box 76009, Nea Smyrni 17110
www.clayart-international.com

Italy

Ceramica Italiana Nell'Edilizia
Via Firenze 276, 48018 Faenza

Japan

Honoho Geijitsu
Abe Corporation, 4-30-12 Kamimeguro
Meguro-ku, Tokyo, 153

Korea

Ceramic Art Monthly
1502-12 Seocho 3dong, Seocho-ku, Seoul
Tel. 02 597 8261 2
Fax 02 597 8039

Netherlands

Keramiek
Poeldijk 8, 3646 AW Waverveen

Klei (until 7/96 called 'Klei & Hobby')
Marterlaan 13, 6705 CK Wageningen
Tel. 0317 42 5802
Fax. 0317 41 2990

Stook
Laan 22, 1741 EB Schagen

Spain

Bulleti Informatiu de Ceramica
Sant Honorat 7, Barcelona 08002

Taiwan

Ceramic Art
PO Box 47-74, Taipei

Useful Web Sites

CERAM Research Ltd,
www.ceram.co.uk/index.html
Ceramic Sculpture
www.ceramicsculpture.com
Ceramica On Line site of Faenza
www.italian-ceramics.com

Ceramics Today
www.ceramicstoday.com

Ceramics Web.
grafik.sdsu.edu/index.html

Clay Worker's Ring
dir.webring.com/rw

ClayArt. Internet Discussion Group
www.ceramics.org/clayart

Claynet
www.ceramicstoday.com

Claystation..
www.claystation.com

GlazeExchange
www.glazeexchange.com/topFrame.php3

ImagineCeramic.
www.ceramique.com

International Academy of Ceramics
www.aic-iac.org

Interpreting Ceramics- University of Wales Inst. Cardiff
www.uwic.ac.uk/ICRC/archives.htm

Rufford Ceramic Centre
www.ruffordceramiccentre.org.uk

SDSU CeramicsWeb
art.sdsu.edu/ceramicsweb

Studio Pottery.
www.studiopottery.co.uk

General Suppliers of all Materials and Equipment

United Kingdom

Bath Potters' Supplies
2 Dorset Close, East Twerton,
Bath BA2 3RF.
Tel. 01223 337046,
www.bathpotters.demon.co.uk

Briar Wheels and Supplies Ltd.
Whitsbury Rd, Fordingbridge,
Hants SP6 1NQ.
Tel. 01425 652991,
www.briarwheels.co.uk

Ceramatech Ltd.
Unit 16, Frontier Works,
33 Queen Street, London N17 8JA

Tel. 020 8885 4492

Clayman
Morells Barn, Park Lane, Lagness,
Chichester, West Sussex. PO20 1LR
Tel. 01243 265845
www.claymansupplies.co.uk

Potclays Ltd
Brickkiln Lane, Etruria,
Stoke-on-Trent ST4 7BP.
Tel. 01782 219816
www.potclays.co.uk

Potterycrafts/Reward-Clayglaze Ltd.
Campbell Rd, Stoke-on-Trent ST4 4ET.
www.potterycrafts.co.uk

Scarva Pottery Supplies.
Unit 20, Scarva Road, Banbridge,
County Down BT32 3QD.
Tel. 018206 69699
www.scarvapottery.com

United States of America

American Art Clay Co Inc (Amaco)
Brent Pottery Equipment Genesis Artist
Colors International 6060 Guion Road
Indianapolis, IN 46254-1222
Tel.317-244-6871
www.amaco.com

Axner Pottery Supply
490 Kane Court, Oviedo,
Florida 32765
www.axner.com

BigCeramicStore.Com
881 E Glendale, Sparks NV
www.bigceramicstore.com

The Chinese Clay Art
www.chineseclayart.com

Leslie Ceramics Supply Co
1212 San Pablo Ave, Berkeley,
CA 94706.
Tel. 510 524 7363
www.leslieceramics.com

Seattle Pottery Supply
35 South Hanford, Seattle, WA 98134
Tel. 206 587 0570
www.seattlepotterysupply.com
Email info@seattlepotterysupply.com

Standard Ceramic Supply Co
Box 4435, Pittsburgh, PA 15205.
Tel. 412 276 6333
www.standardceramic.com

Canada

Tucker's Pottery Supplies Inc
15 West Pearce St, Unit 7, Richmond Hill,
Ontario L4B 1H6.
Tel. 905 889 7705
www.tuckerspottery.com
Greenbarn Potters Supply Ltd.
9548 - 192nd Street, Surrey, B.C. V4N 3R9
www.greenbarn.com

Australia

Clayworks Australia
6 Johnston Court, Dandenong,
Victoria 3175
www.clayworksaustralia.com
Potters Equipment
42 New Street, Ringwood, Victoria 3134
Tel. 03 9870 75533
www.pottersequip.citysearch.com.au
Pottery Supplies
262 Given Tce, Paddington,
Brisbane QLD 4064
Tel. 07 36 3633
www.potterysupplies.com.au

Germany

Keramic-Kraft
Industriestr.28 – D-91227
Diepersdorf b. Nürnberg

France

Cigale et Fourmi
84, rue de Condé 59000 Lille France
www.cigaleetfourmi.fr

Netherlands

Keramicos
153 2031 CC HAARLEM
Tel. 023 542 44 16
Email info@keramikos.nl
www.keramikos.nl

Specialist Suppliers of Clay and Materials

United Kingdom

W. G. Ball Ltd
Longton Mill, Anchor Rd, Longton,
Stoke-on-Trent 5T3 1JW
Tel. 01782 312286
www.wgball.com
Commercial Clay Ltd
Sandbach Road Cobridge,
Stoke-on-Trent. ST4 2DR
www.commercialclay.co.uk
CTM Supplies Ltd
9 Unit 1B, Millpark Industrial Estate,
White Cross Road, Woodbury
Salterton EX5 1EL
www.ctmsupplies.co.uk
W. J. Doble Pottery Clays
Newtowns Sand and Clay Pits, St. Agnes,
Cornwall TR5 0ST
Tel. 01872 552979
Spencroft Ceramics Ltd
Spencroft Rd, Holditch Ind. Est,
Newcastle, Staffs, STS 9JB
Tel. 01782 627004
Valentine Clays
The Sliphouse, 18-20 Chell Street,
Hanley, Stoke-on-Trent. ST1 6BA
www.valentineclays.co.uk

United States of America

Aardvark Clay & Supplies Inc.
1400 E. Pomona Street, Santa Ana,
CA 92705
Tel. 714 541 4157
www.aardvarkclay.com
A.R.T. Studio Clay Company, Inc.
9320 Michigan Avenue Sturtevant,
WI 53177-2435
Tel.708 593 6060
www.artclay.com
Big Bear Alaskan Clay Works
Perkins Dr Fairbanks, AK
Tel. 907 479 2020 2008
Industrial Minerals Company
7268 Frasinetti Road, Sacramento
CA 95828
www.clayimco.com

Minnesota Clay Co
8001 Grand Ave South, Bloomington,
MN55420
Tel. 800 328 9380
www.minnesotaclayusa.com

Australia
Clayworks Australia
6 Johnston Court Dandenong,
Victoria 3175
www.clayworksaustralia.com
The Pugmill Pty Ltd
17A Rose St. Mile End,
South Australia 5031
Tel. 08 8443-4544
www.pugmill.com.au

Canada
Plainsman Clays Ltd.
Box 1266, 702 Wood Street,
Medicine Hat, Alberta, T1A 7M9
www.plainsmanclays.com
Pottery Supply House
P.O. Box 192, 1120 Speers Rd, Oakville,
Ontario L6L 2X4

Suppliers of Pottery Equipment

United Kingdom
CTM Supplies Ltd
9 Unit 1B, Millpark Industrial Estate,
White Cross Road,
Woodbury Salterton EX5 1EL
www.ctmsupplies.co.uk
Gladstone Eng. Co Ltd
Foxley Lane, Milton,
Stoke-on-Trent ST2 7EH
Tel. 01782-536615
www.gladstone-engineering.com
Hancock Pottery Engineers
Unit 4-6 Brookside Business Park,
Cold Meece, Stone, Staffs.
Tel. 01785 761322
Potters' Mate (*Lotus Wheelhead*)
Cust Hall, Toppesfield, Halstead,
Essex C09 4EB.

Tel. 01787 237 704
www.pottersmate.co.uk
Rayefco Wheels
Longfield Bulstrode Lane, Felden,
Hemel Hempstead,
Hertfordshire HP3 0BP
Tel 01442 242332
www.rayefco.co.uk
Stow Potters' Wheels
4 Brocregin, Llangrannog,
Llandysul. SA44 6AG
Tel. 01239 654300
Email stowwheels@aol.com

United States of America
Bluebird Manufacturing Inc.
P.O. Box 2307, Fort Collins,
Colorado 80522
Tel. 970 484 3243
www.bluebird-mfg.com
Brent Pottery Equipment
6060 Guion Road Indianapolis,
IN 46254-1222
Tel.317 244 6871
www.amaco.com
Kickwheel Pottery Supply
1986 Tucker Industrial Road, Tucker,
Georgia 30084
Tel. 800 241 1895
www.kickwheel.com
Shimpo Ceramics
1701 Glenlake Avenue, Itasca,
Illinois 60143
Tel. 800 237 7079
www.shimpoceramics.com
Soldner Equipment
Muddy Elbow Mfg 310 West 4th Street
Newton, KS 67114
Tel. 316 281 9132
www.soldnerequipment.com

Australia
Clayworks Australia
6 Johnston Court Dandenong,
Victoria 3175
www.clayworksaustralia.com
Venco Products, G.P. & G.F. Hill Pty Ltd,
29 Owen Rd, Kelmscott, WA 6111
Tel. 09 399 5265

www.venco.com.au
Walker Ceramics
45 Tramore Place,
Killarney Heights.Sydney
Tel. 02 9451 5855
www.walkerceramics.com.au

Canada
Ceramics Canada Bay 152,
2880 - 45th Avenue,
SE Calgary, AB T2B 3M1
Tel. 403 255 1575
www.ceramicscanada.net
Pottery Supply House
1120 Speers Road, Oakville,
Ontario, L6L 2X4
Tel. 1 800 465 8544
www.pshcanada.com

New Zealand
Coastal Ceramics: Pottery and Ceramics
Supplies, Unit 3, 7 Omahi St Waikanae
Tel. 04 902 5542
Email coastalceramics@paradise.net.nz

Germany
Helmut Rohde GmbH, Rosenheimer
Straße 89 D-83134 Prutting
Tel. (0)8036/67 49 76 -10
Roderveld
www.roderveld.com/

South Africa
Potters Equipment Factory 13
42 New St, Ringwood, VIC 3134.
www.pottersequip.citysearch.com.au
Potters Supply and Mail Order On-line
www.potters.co.za

Specialist Suppliers of Kilns and Kiln-building Materials

United Kingdom
Acme Batt Co.
Walter Brayford, Grove Cottage, Clay
Lake, Endon, Stoke-on-Trent,
Staffordshire ST9 9DE.

Tel. 01782 505405
Email walter@claylake.com
Barter Burners. Tex Engineering Ltd.
Unit 35 Claydon Business Park,
Great Blakenham, Ipswich IP6 ONL.
Tel. 0870 751 3977
www.barterburners.co.uk
Cromartie Kilns Ltd.
Dept CR, Park Hall Rd, Longton,
Stoke-on-Trent ST3 SAY.
Tel. 01782-313947,
www.cromartie.co.uk.
GHS Refractories Ltd.
Tingley Bar Industrial Estate,
Morley, Leeds. LS27 OHE.
Tel. 0113 252 7144
www.ghsrefractories.co.uk
Kilncare,
30 Norbury Ave, Stoke-on-Trent ST2 7BJ
Tel. 01782 535915
www.kilncare.co.uk
Kilns and Furnaces Ltd.
Keele St, Stoke-on-Trent,
Staffs ST6 5AS
Tel. 01782 344620
www.kilns.co.uk
Laser Kilns Ltd.
Unit 9, Angel Rd Works, Advent Way
London N18 3AH.
Tel. 020 8807 2888
www.laser-kilns.co.uk
Northern Kilns
Pilling Pottery School Lane
Pilling Nr. Garstang,
Lancashire PR3 6HB
Tel. 01253 790307
www.northernkilns.com
Roman Instruments. (*kiln elements and controller repair, Bath*)
Tel. 01225 833427
Stanton Kilns.
Foley Goods Yard, King St, Fenton,
Stoke-on-Trent,
Staffordshire, ST4 3DE
www.stanton-kilns.co.uk
Stedmark Limited. (*gas burners*)
Unit 11, Derby Road Industrial Estate,
Heanor, Derbyshire DE75 7QL
Tel.01773 713300
www.stedmark.com

United States of America

Alpine Kilns
    9320 Michigan Avenue,
    Sturtevant,
    WI 53177-2435
    www.alpinekilns.com

Geil Kilns
    7201 Clay Avenue, Huntington Beach,
    CA 92648
    www.kilns.com

Olsen Kiln Kits
    Pinyon Crest, Box 205, Mountain Center,
    CA 92561.
    Tel.619 349 3291
    www.olsenkilns.com

Paragon Industries
    2011 South Town East Boulevard,
    Mesquite, Texas 75149-1122
    Tel.1 800 876 4328
    www.paragonweb.com

Skutt Ceramic Products
    2618 S.E. Steele St, Portland, OR 97202
    Tel.503 231 7726
    www.skutt.com

Ward Burner Systems
    PO Box 1086 - Dandridge, TN 37725
    Tel. 865 397 2914
    www.wardburner.com

Australia

Craftek Pty Ltd.
    11/31 Shearson Crescent, Mentone,
    Vic, 3194
    Tel. 61 3 9583 9463
    www.craftek.com.au

Port-o-Kiln Pty Ltd.
    36 Brooklyn Ave, Dandenong, Vic 3175
    Tel. 791 6918

Canada

Inproheat
    680 Raymur Ave, Vancouver, B.C.
    Tel. 604 254 0461

Sugar Creek Industries.Inc.
    P.O. Box 354, Linden, IN 47955
    Tel. 1 765 339 4641
    www.sugarcreekind.com

South Africa

Kiln Contracts (Pty).
    Ltd 11 Celie Road, Retreat,
    Cape Town. 7945
    Tel.+27 21 701 6682

Refraline (Pty.) Ltd. (*kiln shelves*)
    P. O. Box 8393 Edenglen 1613
    Tel. 011 392 0700
    www.refraline.com

Suppliers of Kiln Instruments and Cones

United Kingdom

Celtic Kilncare Ltd.
    Celtic Hse, Langland Way,
    Newport NP9 OPT.
    Tel. 01633-271455

The Industrial Pyrometer Co Ltd.
    66-76 Gooch St, Birmingham BS 6QY
    Tel. 0121 622 3511
    www.ipco.co.uk

Stafford Instruments Ltd.
    Unit 22, Wolseley Court Staffordshire
    Technology Park, Stafford ST18 0GA
    Tel. 01785 255588
    www.stafford-inst.co.uk

Taylor Tunnicliff Ltd
    (*Buller's rings and Harrison cones*)
    Uttoxeter Rd, Longton, Stoke-on-Trent
    Tel. 01782 399922
    www.taylortunnicliff.com
    distributed by Potterycrafts Ltd and others.

United States of America

The Edward Orton Jr. Ceramic Foundation
    6991 Old 3C Highway, P.O. Box 460,
    Westerville, Ohio 43081-0460
    Tel. 614 895 2663
    www.ortonceramic.com

W. P. Dawson Inc (*Kiln Sitter*)
    399 Thor Place, Brea, CA 92621
    Tel. 714 529 2813
    www.kiln-sitter.com

FireRight/Warner Instruments
    P.O. Box 604, Grand Haven, MI 49417
    Tel. 616 842 7658
    www.fireright.com

Suppliers of Computer Programs

United Kingdom

Brian Sutherland.
homepage.ntlworld.com/psutherland/briansutherland/Pages/tribase.htm
David Hewitt,
7 Fairfield Rd, Newport NP6 1DQ
John B. May,
19 Church Rd, Boldmere,
Sutton Coldfield B73 SRX
www.dhpot.demon.co.uk/CeramDat.htm

United States of America

GlazeMaster. Frog Pond Pottery
P.O. Box 88, Pocopson,
PA 19366-0088
www.masteringglazes.com
Hyperglaze. R. Burkctt,
6354 Lorca Drive, San Diego,
CA 92115-5509
www.hyperglaze.com
GlazeChem Robert J. Wilt
542 Erickson Rd., Ashby MA 01431
www.dinoclay.com
Glaze Software. The Ceramics Web.
http://grafik.sdsu.edu/glazesoftware.html

Canada

Insight. Tony Hansen Digitalfire Corporation
Box 432, Cornwall, PE, C0A 1H0
Tel. 403 668 0590
www.digitalfire.com

New Zealand

Matrix. Lawrence Ewing,
10 Aurora Terrace, Port Chalmers
www.matrix2000.co.nz

Suppliers of Safety Equipment

Metrosales (TCAS), Surrey
Suppliers of ceramics safety equipment
Tel. 020 8546 1108
Email sales@metrosales.co.uk.

The Safety Site.
PO Box 30479, London NW6 6FY
www.thesafetysite.co.uk

Suppliers of Films and Videos

Concord Video & Film Council
Rosehill Centre, 22 Hines Road, Ipswich,
Suffolk IP3 9BG UK
www.concordvideo.co.uk
Crawdad Documentary, North Carolina, US
www.folkfilms.com
Custom Fix - Video Shop. African Potters.
www.customflix.com
International Catalogue of Films on
Ceramics, Kalkspatz Guenter Haltmayer,
Dorfstr. 14, D-17194 Klein Luckow,
Tel.+49-39933-71695
www.kalkspatz.ceramic.de
Marty Gross Productions, Inc.- Potters Films
including Leach and others
www.martygrossfilms.com
Films for Potters -John Anderson, East View,
The Green, Long Melford, Sudbury,
Suffolk, CO10 9DU UK.
Paul Soldner Playing with Fire [2005]
www.ifilm.com/ifilmdetail/2667063
Queens Row. Revolutions of the Wheel:
The Emergence of Clay Art
www.queensrow.org

Archives

Ceramics Archive, School of Art,
University of Wales, Buarth Mawr,
Aberystwyth, Dyfed SY23 1NE
Tel. 01970 622460
www.aber.ac.uk/~cerwww/
Crafts Council 44a - Resources. Pentonville
Road, Islington, London N1 9BY
Tel. +44 020 7278 7700
www.craftscouncil.org.uk
NEVAC National Electronic and Video
Àrchive of the Crafts
www.media.uwe.ak.uk/nevac

Bibliography

Books on Ceramics – all aspects

D. Billington, revised J. Colbeck, *The Techniques of Pottery* (Batsford 1975).

B. Blandino, *Coiled Pottery* (A & C Black; Krause, Craftsman House 1997)

R. C. Brodie, *The Energy Efficient Potter* (Watson-Guptill 1983)

M. Cardew, *Pioneer Pottery* (A & C Black; The American Ceramic Society 2002)

M. Casson, *The Craft of the Potter* (BBC Publications 1979)

J. Colbeck, *The Technique of Throwing* (Batsford 1969)

J. Colbeck, *Pottery Materials* (Batsford 1988)

E. Cooper, *Electric Kiln Pottery* (Batsford 1982)

J. Doherty, *Porcelain* (A & C Black; University of Pennsylvania Press 2002)

M. and V. Eden *Slipware* (A & C Black; University of Pennsylvania Press; Craftsman House 1999)

R. Fournier, *Illustrated Dictionary of Practical Pottery* 3rd ed (A & C Black; Krause; Craftsman House 1992)

F. and J. Hamer, *The Potter's Dictionary of Materials and Techniques* (A & C Black; University of Pennsylvania Press; Craftsman House 1997)

A. Holden, *The Self-Reliant Potter* (A & C Black 1982)

J. B. Kenny, *Ceramic Design* (Pitman 1967, Chilton 1963)

B. Leach, *A Potter's Book* (Faber & Faber 1949, Transatlantic 1973)

M. Ostermann, *The Ceramic Surface* (A & C Black; University of Pennsylvania Press 2002)

G. C. Nelson, *Ceramics, a Potter's Handbook* (Holt, Rinehart & Winston 1971)

D. Parks, *A Potter's Guide to Raw Glazing and Oil Firing* (Pitman 1980)

J. Pollex, *Slipware* (Pitman/Watson-Guptill 1979)

A. Reijnders, *The Ceramic Process* (A & C Black; University of Pennslyvania Press 2005)

D. Rhodes, *Stoneware and Porcelain* (Pitman 1960, Chilton 1959)

P. Rogers, *Throwing Pots* (A & C Black; Craftsman House 1995)

T. Shafer, *Pottery Decoration* (Watson-Guptill 1976)

P. Starkey, *Saltglaze* (Pitman/Watson-Guptill 1977)

C. Tyler and R. Hirsch, *Raku Techniques for Contemporary Potters* (Pitman 1975)

R. Zakin, *Electric Kiln Ceramics* 2nd ed (A & C Black, Chilton 1994)

Books on Glazes and Glazing Techniques

Ceramic Review Book of Clays and Glazes (Ceramic Review Publications)

M. Bailey, *Oriental Glazes* (A & C Black; University of Pennsylvania Press, 2004)

P. Beard, *Resist and Masking Techniques* (A & C Black; Craftsman House 1996)

E. Cooper, *The Potter's Book of Glaze Recipes* (Batsford 1980)

G. Daley, *Glazes and Glazing Techniques* (A & C Black; Kangaroo Press 1995)

H. Fraser, *Ceramic Faults and their Remedies* (A & C Black 1986)

H. Fraser, *Glazes for the Craft Potter* (A & C Black; The American Ceramic Society; Craftsman House 1999)

J. Gibson, *Pottery Decoration* (A & C Black; Craftsman House 1997)

Frank and Janet Hamer, *Clays* (Pitman/Watson-Guptill 1977)

R. Hopper, *The Ceramic Spectrum* (Collins; Chilton 1984)

W. G. Lawrence and R. R. West, *Ceramic Science for the Potter* (Chilton 1984)

J. Mansfield, *Salt-Glazed Ceramics* (A & C Black; Craftsman House 1991)

D. Rhodes, *Clay and Glazes for the Potter* 2nd rev. ed (A & C Black; Chilton 1996)

P. Rogers, *Ash Glazes* (A & C Black; University of Pennsylvania Press, 2003)

P. Rogers, *Salt Glazing* (A & C Black; University of Pennsylvania Press, 2002)

B. Sutherland, *Glazes from Natural Sources* (A & C Black, University of Pennsylvania Press 2005)

F. Tristram, *Single Firing* (A & C Black; Craftsman House 1996)

R. Tudball, *Soda Glazing* (A & C Black; Craftsman House 1995)

N. Wood, *Chinese Glazes* (A & C Black; University of Pennsylvania Press; Craftsman House 1999)

N. Wood, *Oriental Glazes* (Pitman/Watson-Guptill 1978)

Books on Kilns and Firing

R. Fournier, *Electric Kiln Construction for Potters* (Van Nostrand Reinhold 1978)

H. Fraser, *Ceramic Faults and Their Remedies* (A & C Black; Gentle Breeze 2005)

H. Fraser, *The Electric Kiln* (A & C Black; Craftsman House 1994)

I. Gregory, *Kiln Building* 2nd edition (A & C Black; Craftsman House 1995)

I. Gregory, *Alternative Kilns* (A & C Black 2005)

N. Lou, *The Art of Firing* (A & C Black; Gentle Breeze 1998)

C. Minogue & R. Sanderson, *Wood-fired Ceramics* (A & C Black 2000)

F. Olsen, *The Kiln Book* 2nd edition (A & C Black, Chilton 1983)

J. Perryman, *Smoke-fired Pottery* (A & C Black; Craftsman House 1995)

D. Rhodes, *Kilns* (Pitman 1969, Chilton 1968)

J. Troy, *Wood-Fired Stoneware and Porcelain* (Chilton 1995)

Health and Safety

Institute of Ceramics: *Health and Safety in Ceramics* (Pergamon 1981)

Institute of Ceramics: *Safety in Ceramic Education*

British Standards Institute, 2 Park Street, London, W1A 2BS, UK

Art Hazards Information Center, 5 Beekman Street, NY 10038, USA

Index